FOR ORGANS, PIANOS & ELECTRONIC KEYBOARDS

E-Z PLAY TODAY

77

— THE —

ANDREW LLOYD WEBBER™
SHEET MUSIC COLLECTION

T0088298

Andrew Lloyd Webber™ is a trademark owned by Andrew Lloyd Webber.

ISBN 978-1-4950-9849-9

HAL•LEONARD®

7777 W. BLUEMOUND RD. P.O. BOX 13819 MILWAUKEE, WI 53213

In Australia Contact:
Hal Leonard Australia Pty. Ltd.
4 Lentara Court
Cheltenham, Victoria, 3192 Australia
Email: ausadmin@halleonard.com.au

Visit Hal Leonard Online at
www.halleonard.com

CONTENTS

All I Ask of You
from THE PHANTOM OF THE OPERA

Registration 3
Rhythm: Ballad

Music by Andrew Lloyd Webber
Lyrics by Charles Hart
Additional Lyrics by Richard Stilgoe

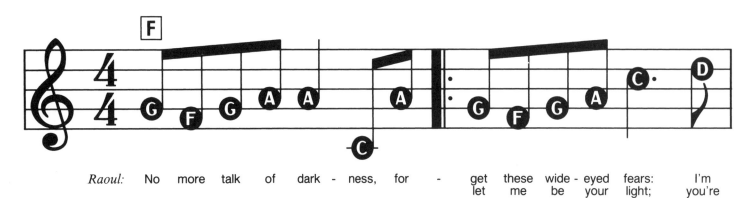

Raoul: No more talk of dark - ness, for - get these wide - eyed fears: I'm
let me be your light; you're

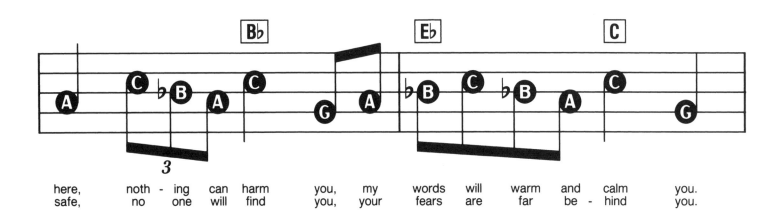

here, noth - ing can harm you, my words will warm and calm you.
safe, no one will find you, your fears are far be - hind you.

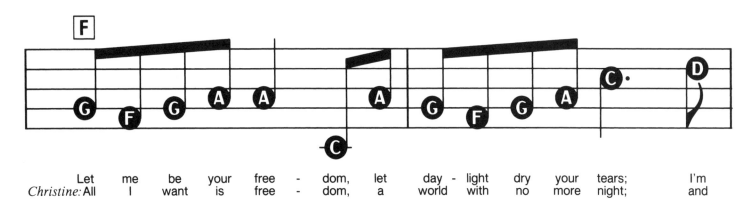

Let me be your free - dom, let day - light dry your tears; I'm
Christine: All I want is free - dom, a world with no more night; and

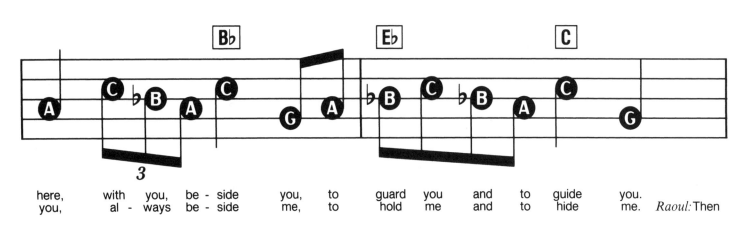

here, with you, be - side you, to guard you and to guide you.
you, al - ways be - side me, to hold me and to hide me. *Raoul:* Then

5

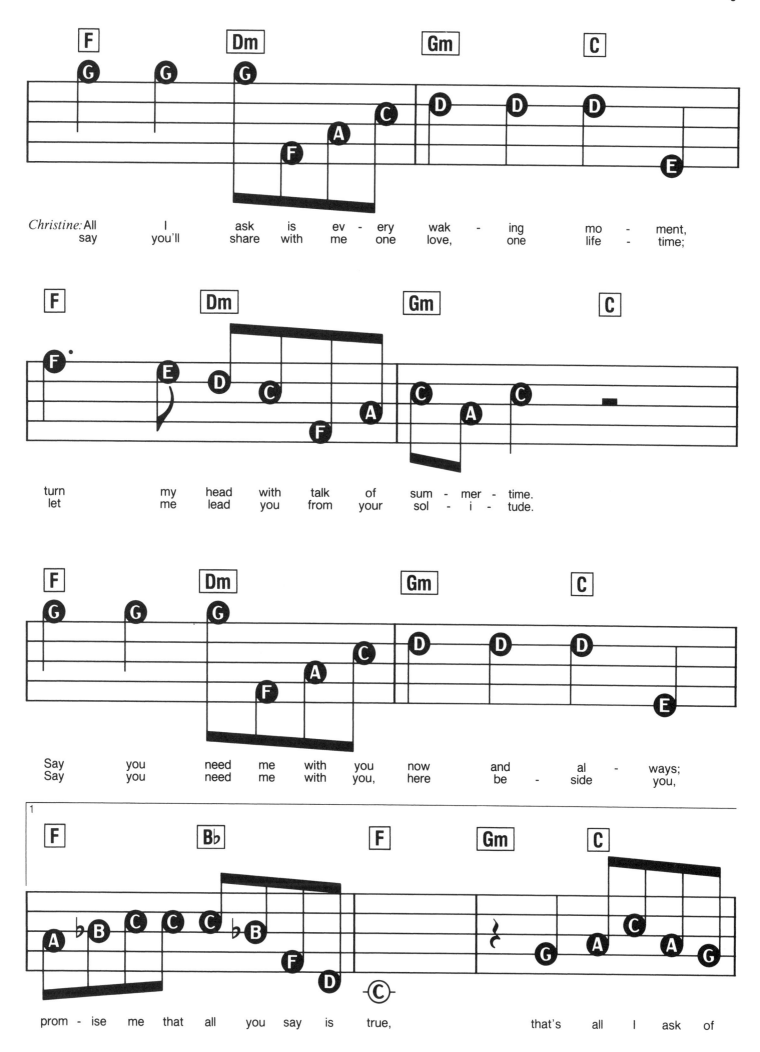

6

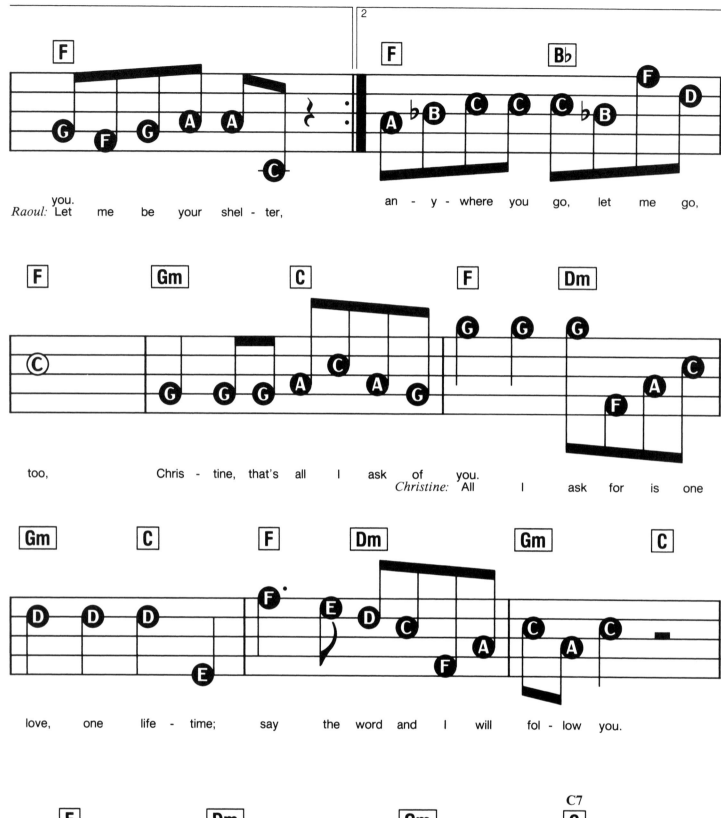

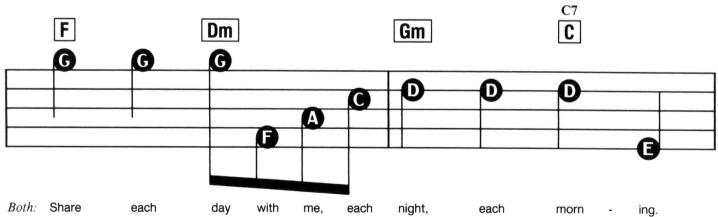

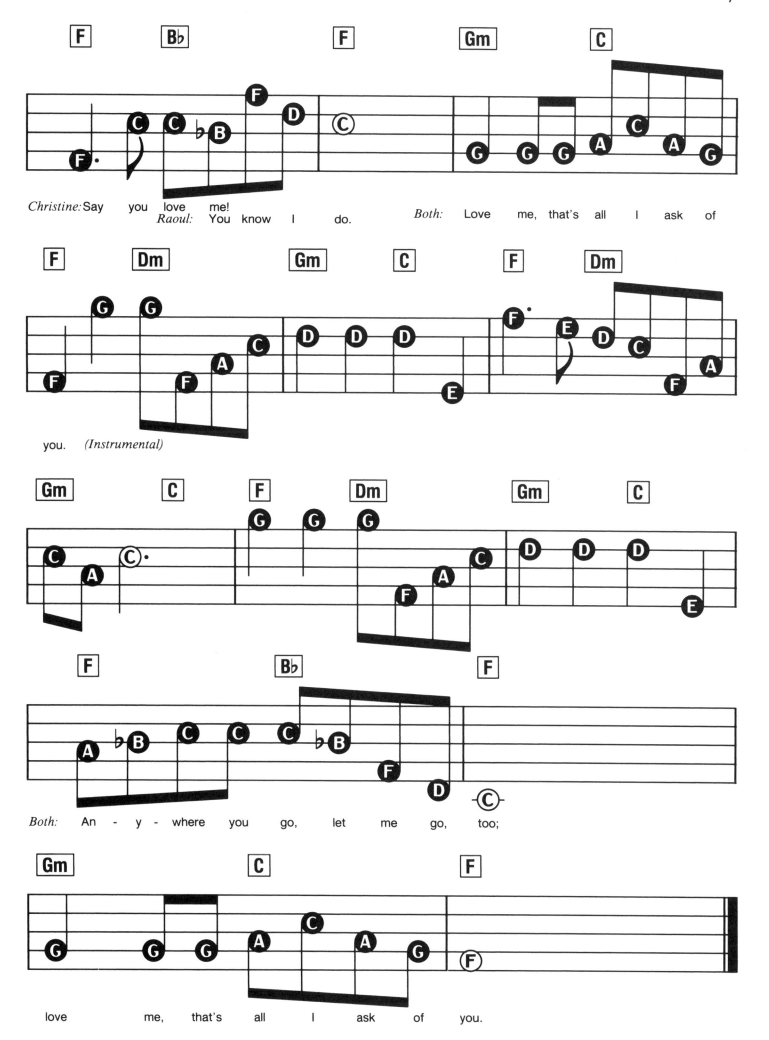

Amigos Para Siempre
(Friends for Life)
The Official Theme of the Barcelona 1992 Games

Registration 3
Rhythm: Bossa Nova or 8-Beat

Music by Andrew Lloyd Webber
Lyrics by Don Black

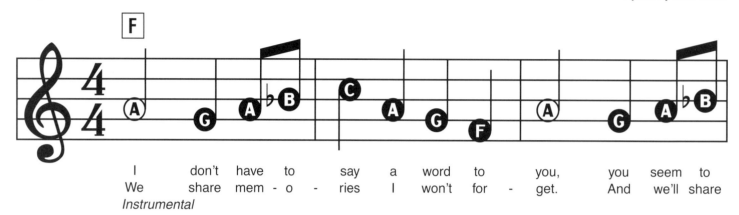

I don't have to say a word to you, you seem to
We share mem - o - ries I won't for - get. And we'll share

Instrumental

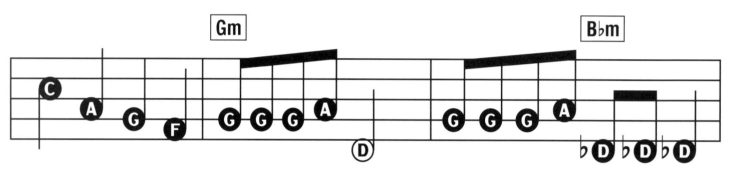

know what - ev - er mood I'm go - ing through. Feel as though I've known you for -
more, my friend, we have - n't start - ed yet. Some-thing hap - pens when we're to -

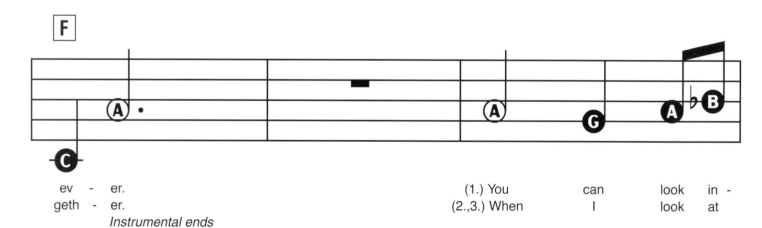

ev - er.
geth - er.

(1.) You can look in -
(2.,3.) When I look at

Instrumental ends

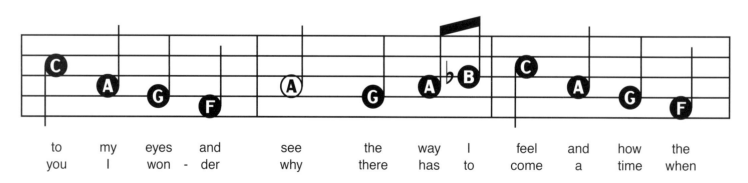

to my eyes and see the way I feel and how the
you I won - der why there has to come a time when

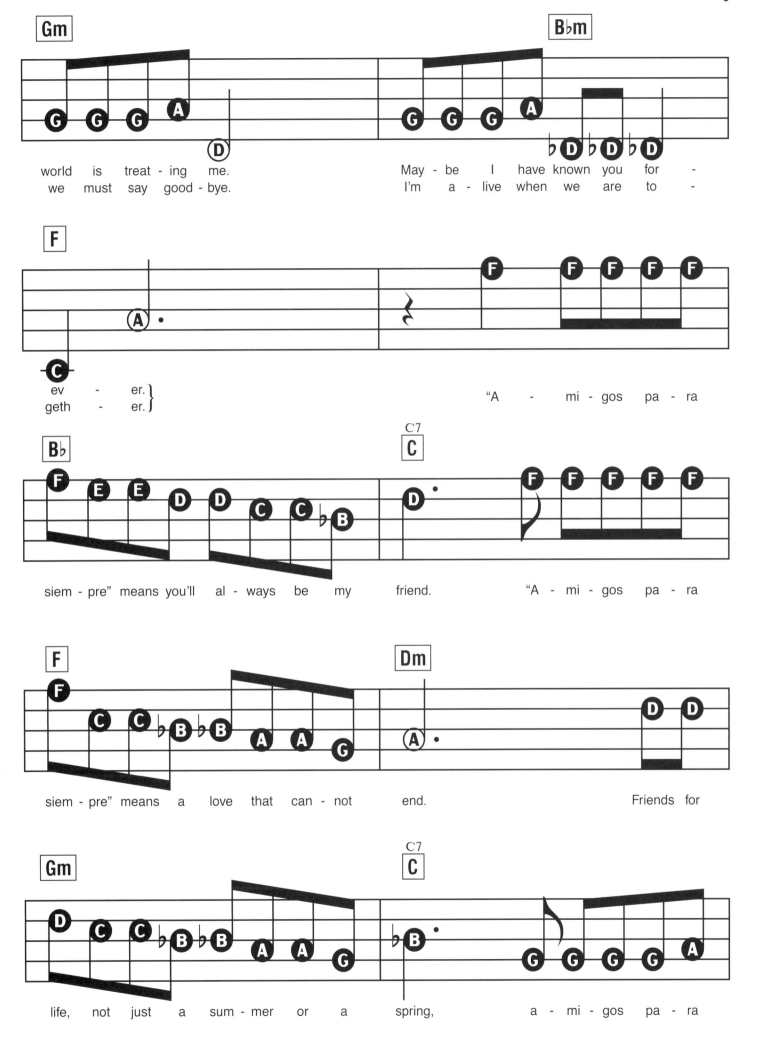

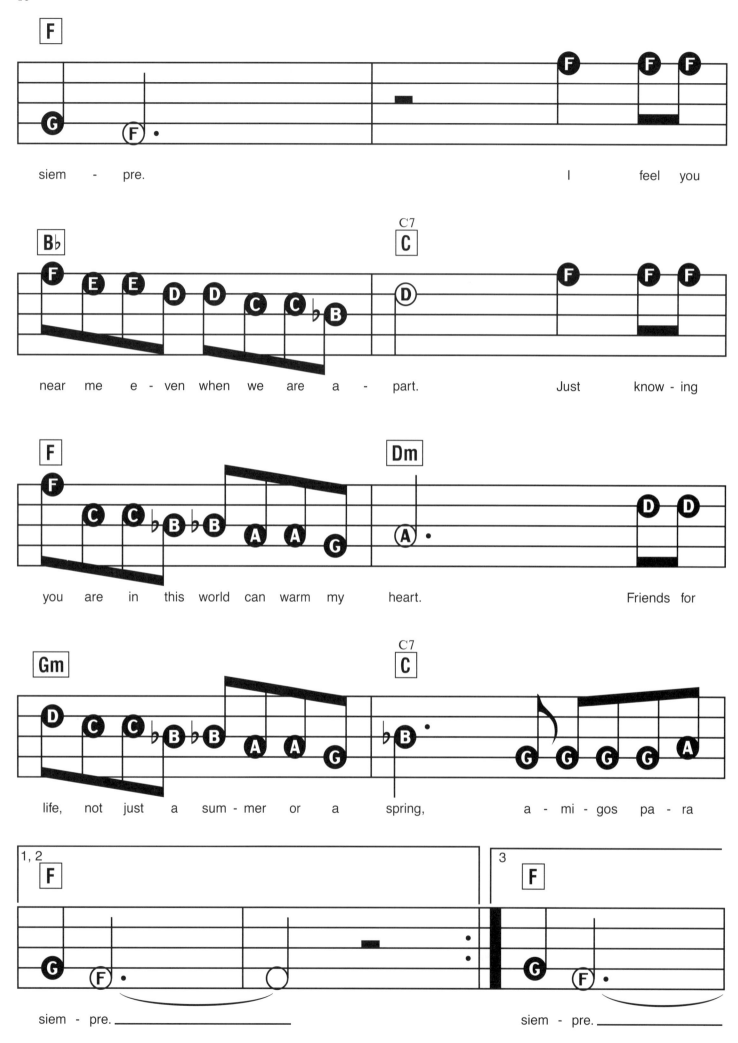

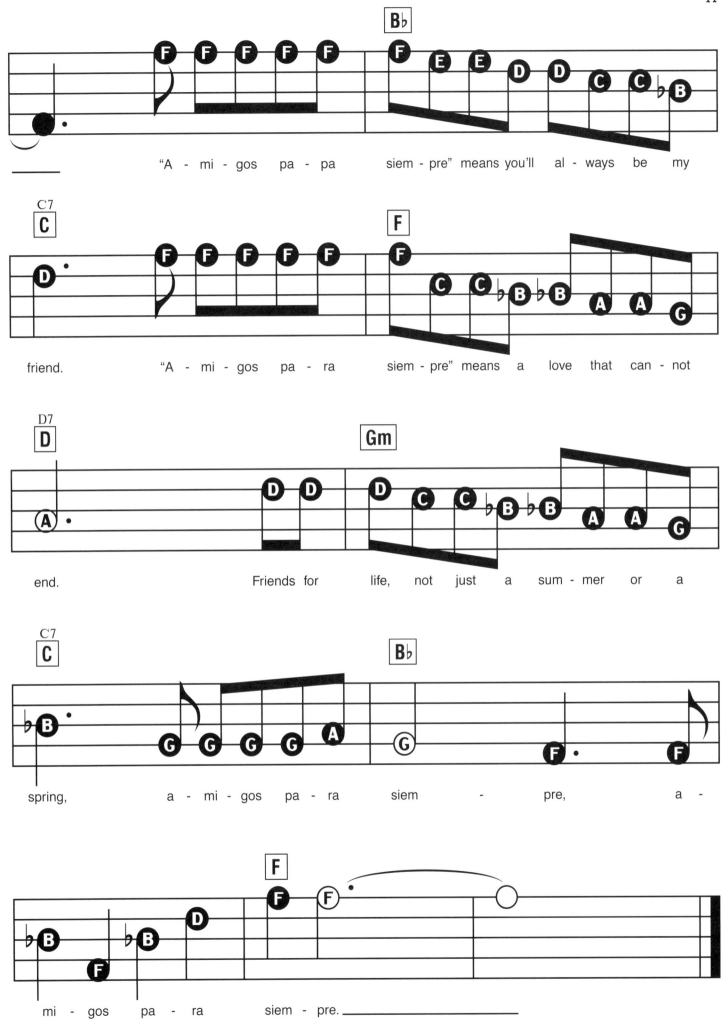

Any Dream Will Do

from JOSEPH AND THE AMAZING TECHNICOLOR® DREAMCOAT

Registration 6
Rhythm: Ballad or Shuffle

Music by Andrew Lloyd Webber
Lyrics by Tim Rice

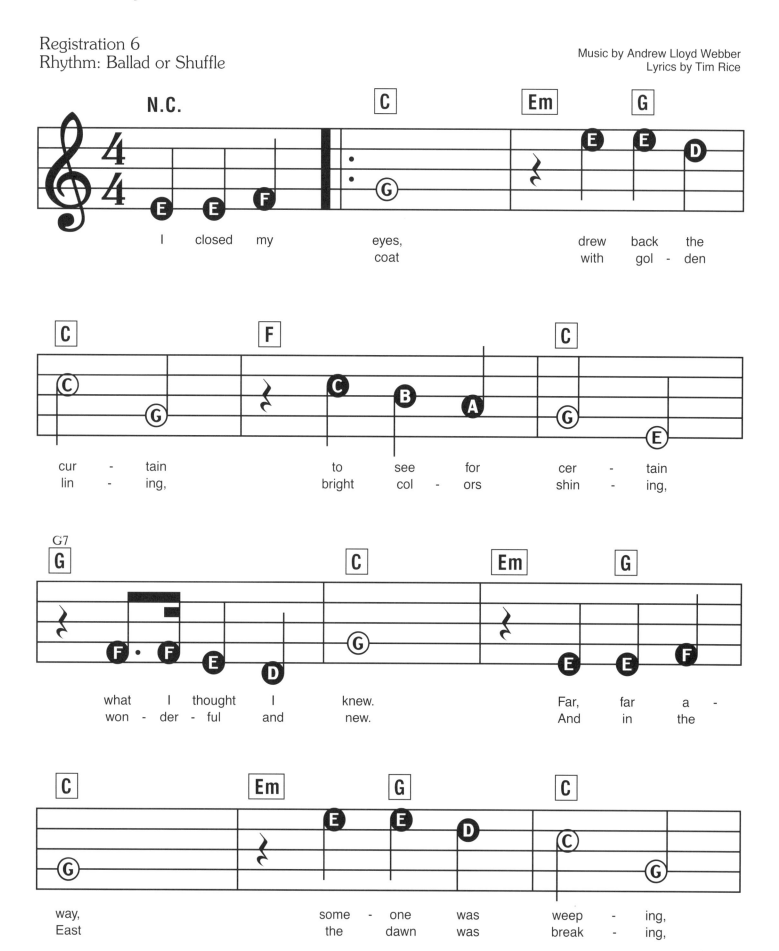

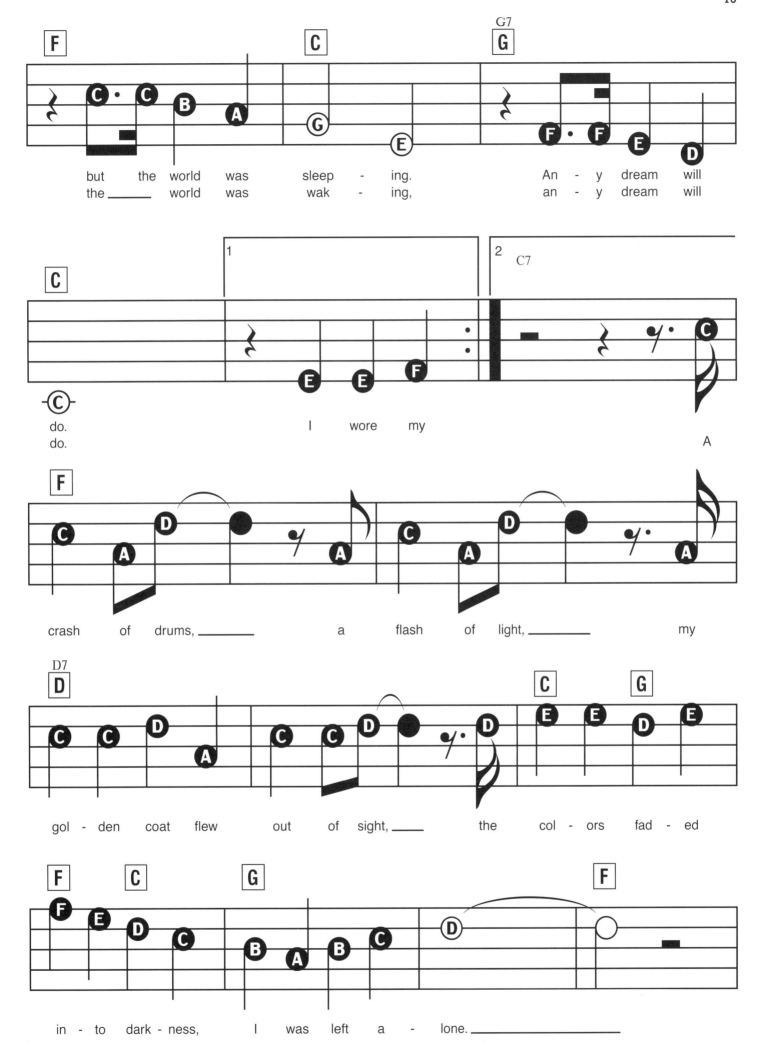

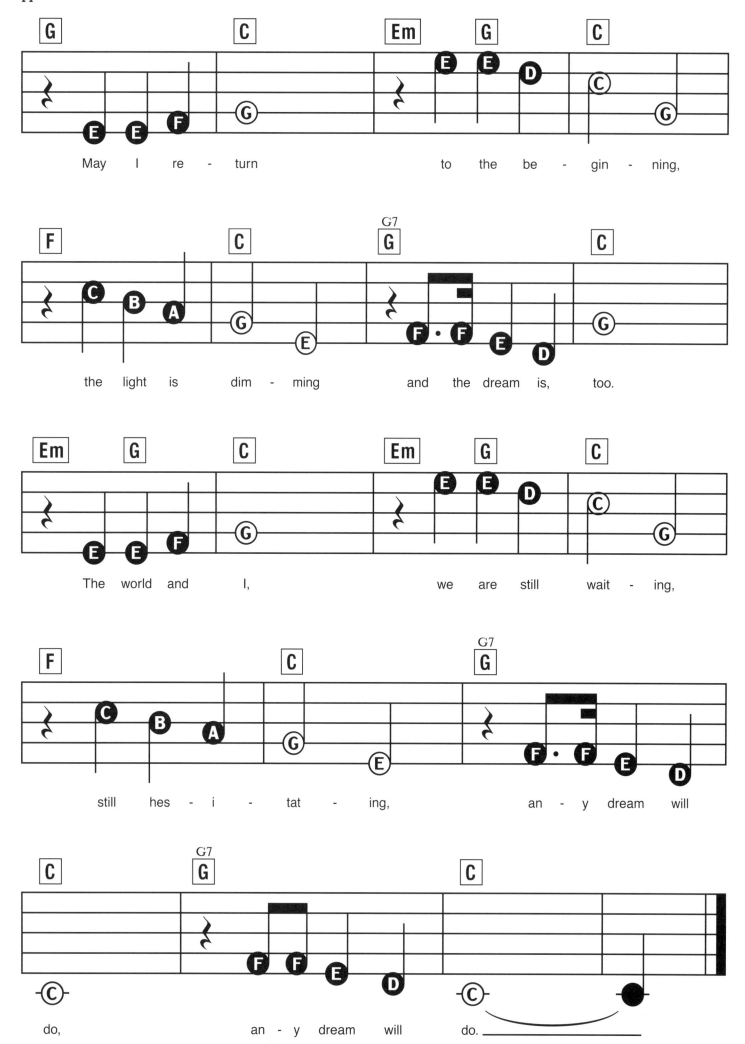

Close Every Door
from JOSEPH AND THE AMAZING TECHNICOLOR® DREAMCOAT

Registration 2
Rhythm: Waltz

Music by Andrew Lloyd Webber
Lyrics by Tim Rice

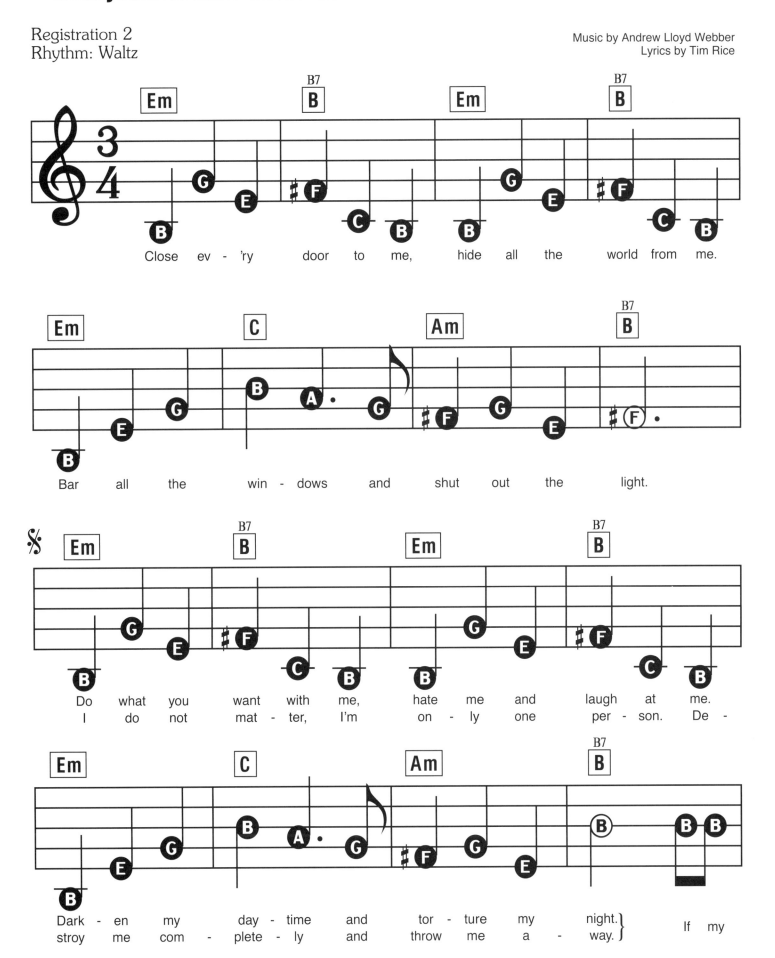

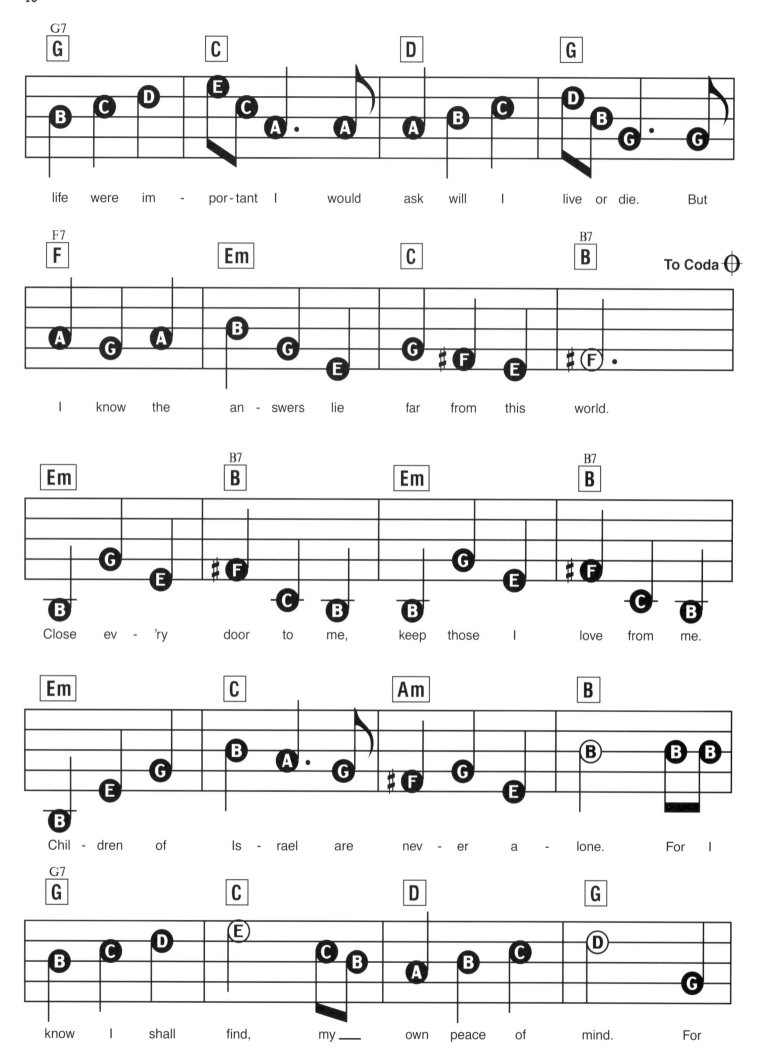

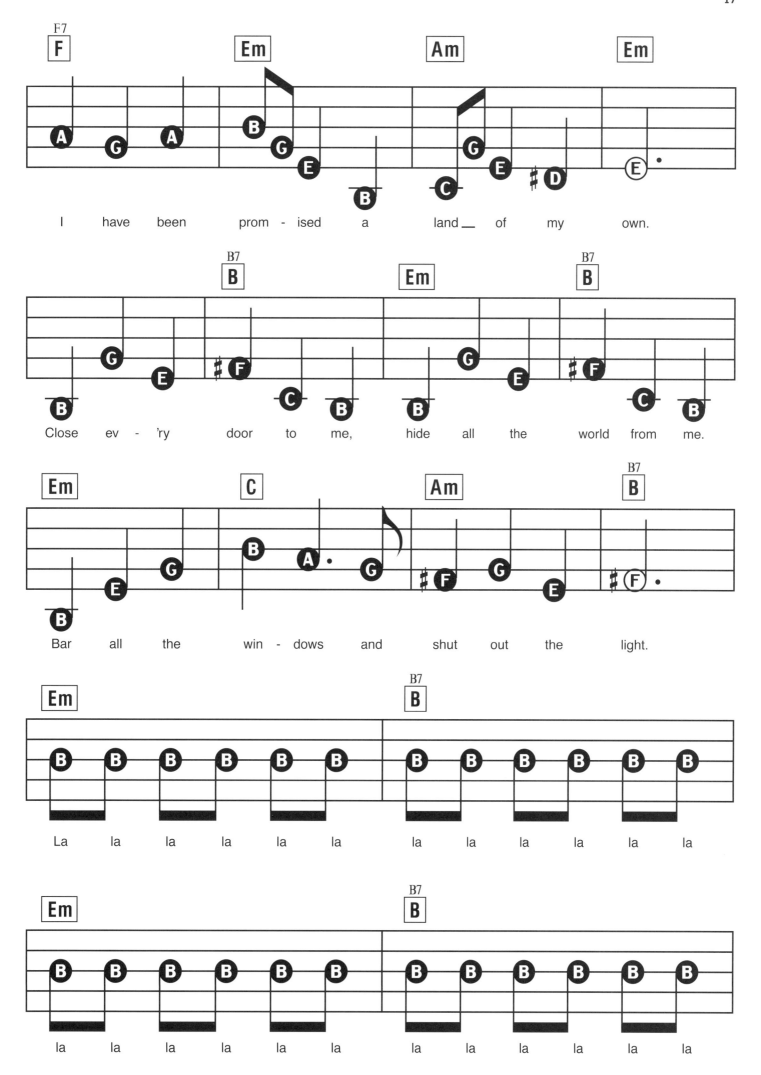

18

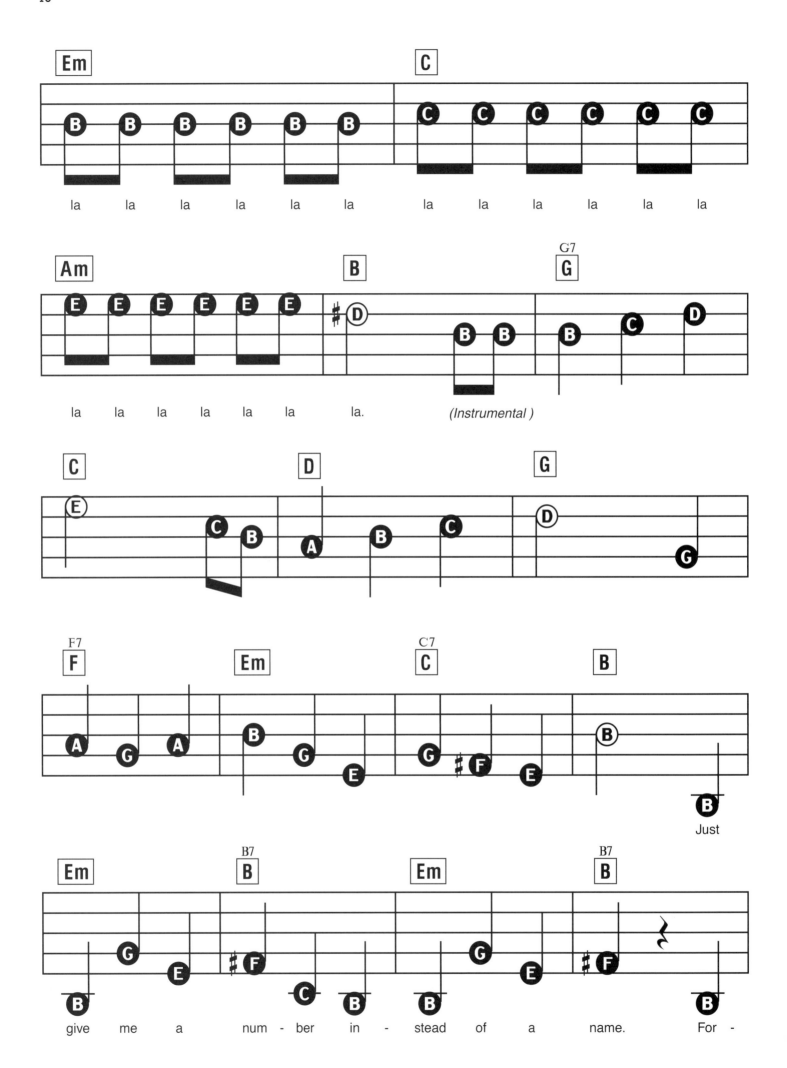

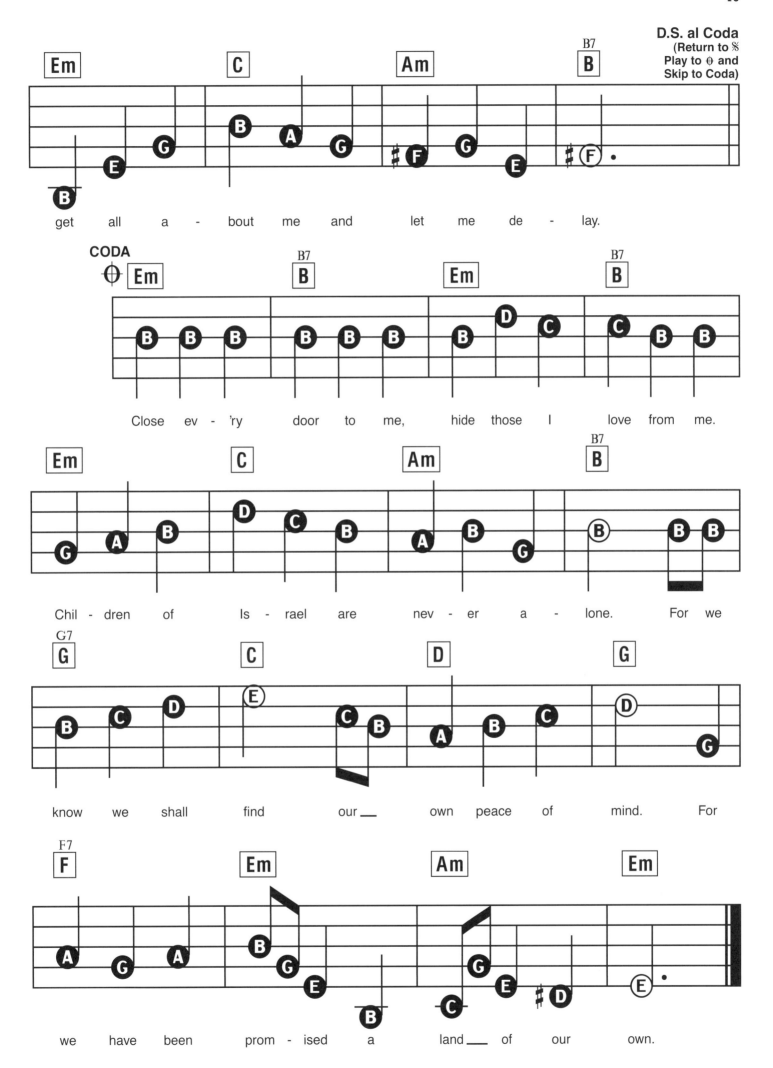

As If We Never Said Goodbye

from SUNSET BOULEVARD

Registration 2
Rhythm: Ballad or 8-Beat

Music by Andrew Lloyd Webber
Lyrics by Don Black and Christopher Hampton
with contributions by Amy Powers

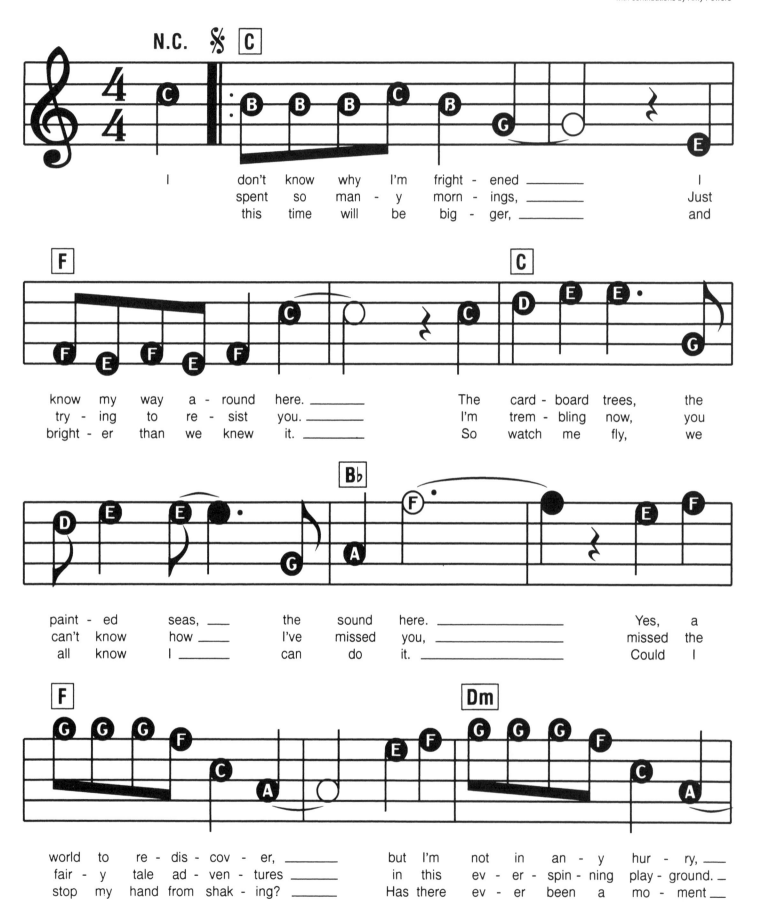

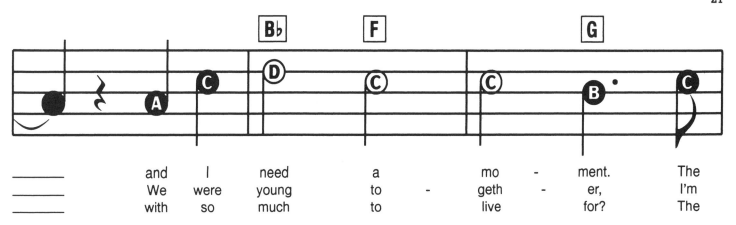

and I need a mo - ment. The
We were young to - geth - er, I'm
with so much to live for? The

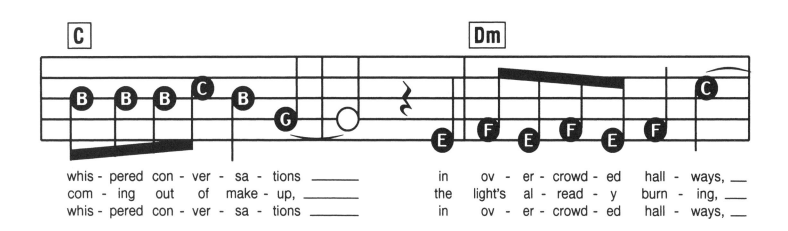

whis - pered con - ver - sa - tions _____ in ov - er - crowd - ed hall - ways, __
com - ing out of make - up, _____ the light's al - read - y burn - ing, __
whis - pered con - ver - sa - tions _____ in ov - er - crowd - ed hall - ways, __

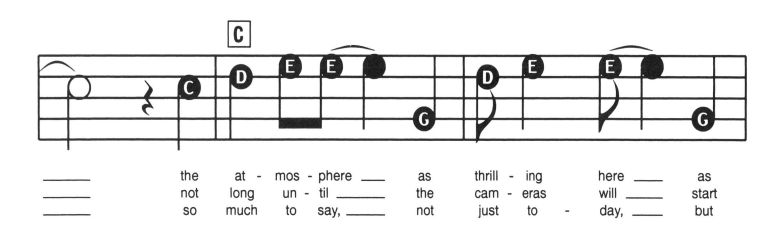

the at - mos - phere ___ as thrill - ing here ___ as
not long un - til _____ the cam - eras will _____ start
so much to say, _____ not just to - day, _____ but

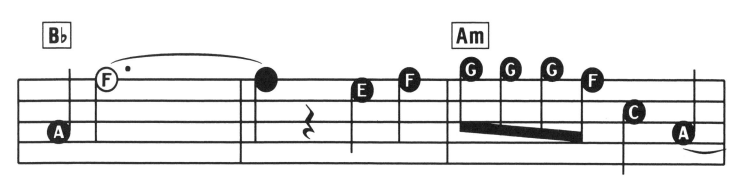

al - ways. _____ Feel the ear - ly morn - ing mad - ness, __
turn - ing, _____ and the ear - ly morn - ing mad - ness __
al - ways. _____ We'll have ear - ly morn - ing mad - ness, __

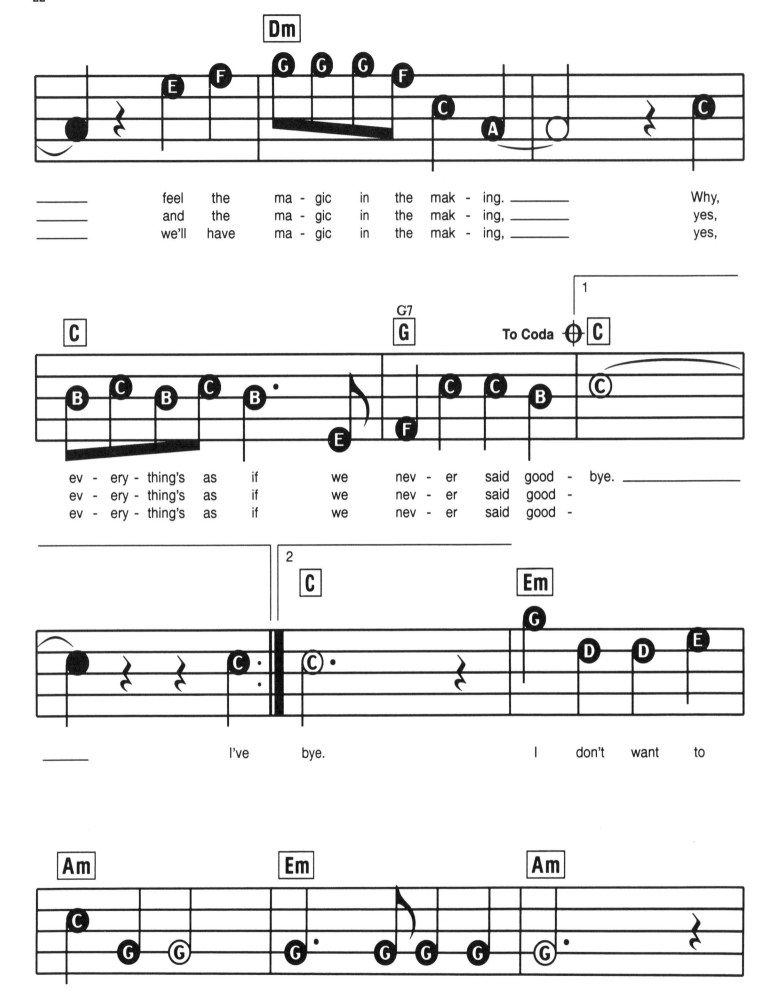

feel the ma - gic in the mak - ing. _____ Why,
and the ma - gic in the mak - ing, _____ yes,
we'll have ma - gic in the mak - ing, _____ yes,

ev - ery - thing's as if we nev - er said good - bye. _____
ev - ery - thing's as if we nev - er said good -
ev - ery - thing's as if we nev - er said good -

_____ I've bye.   I don't want to

be a - lone,   that's all in the past.

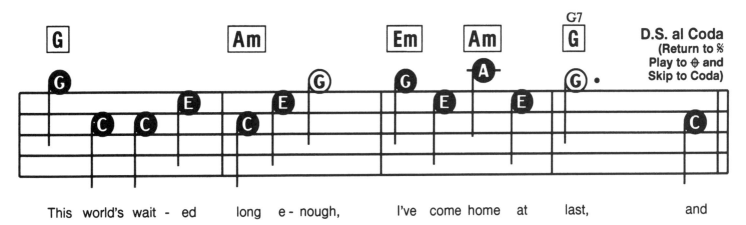

This world's wait - ed long e - nough, I've come home at last, and

D.S. al Coda
(Return to %
Play to ⊕ and
Skip to Coda)

CODA

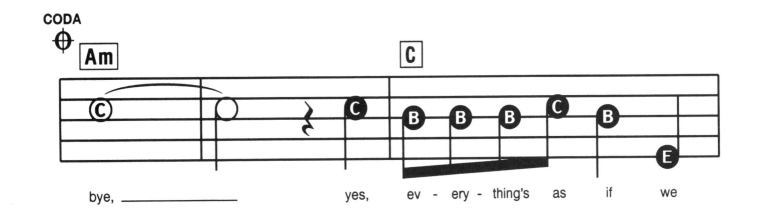

bye, _____ yes, ev - ery - thing's as if we

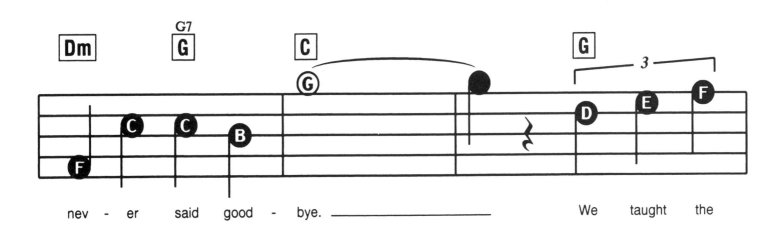

nev - er said good - bye. _____ We taught the

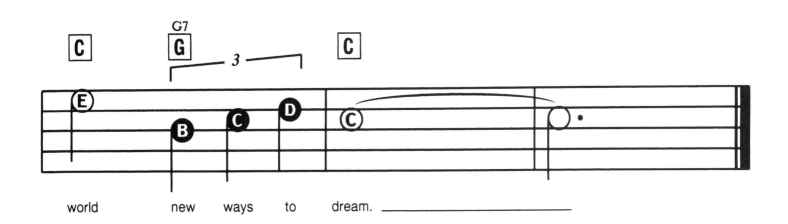

world new ways to dream. _____

Don't Cry for Me Argentina
from EVITA

Registration 9
Rhythm: Ballad

Words by Tim Rice
Music by Andrew Lloyd Webber

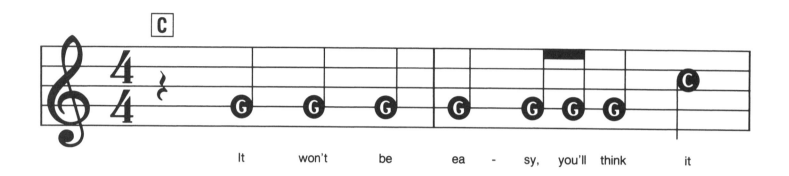

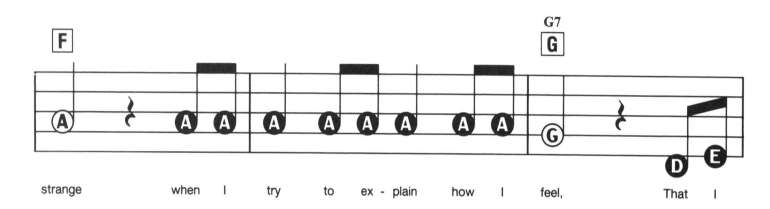

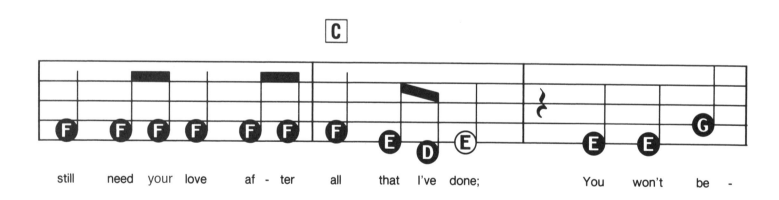

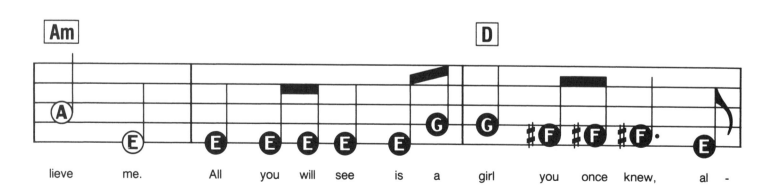

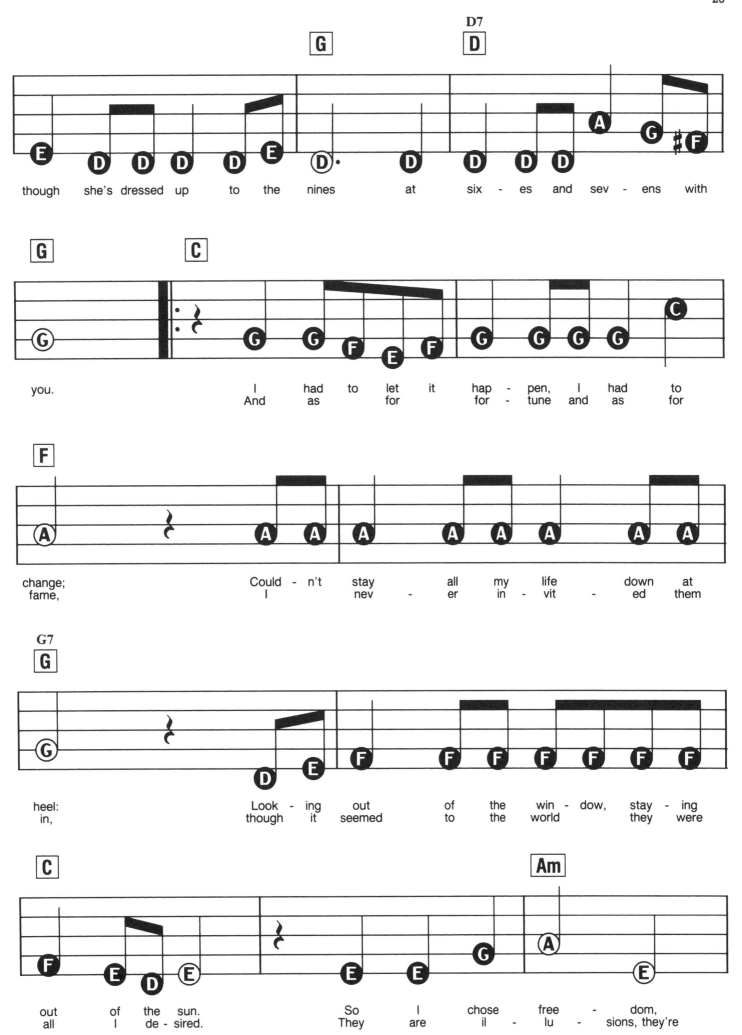

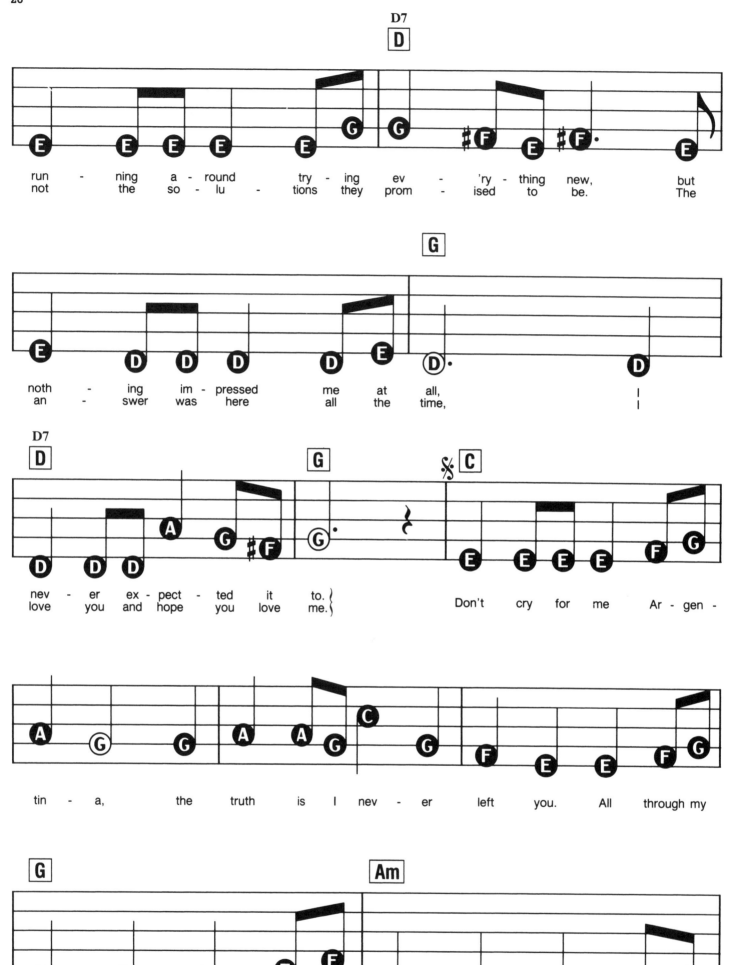

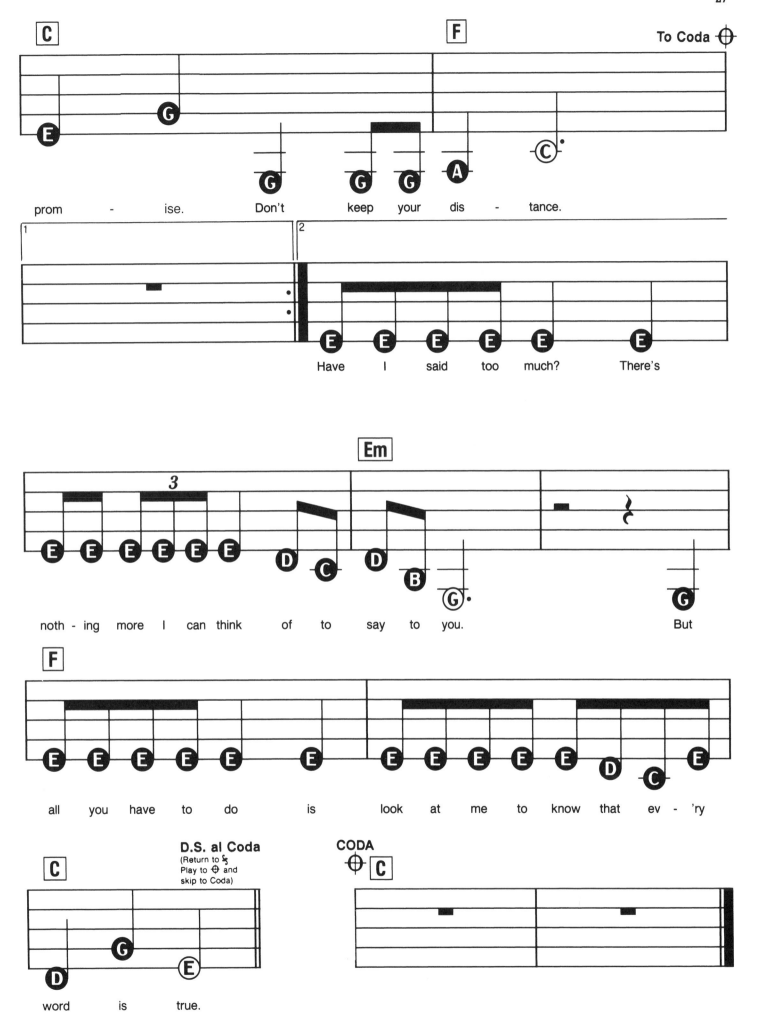

Everything's Alright
from JESUS CHRIST SUPERSTAR

Registration 8
Rhythm: No Rhythm

Words by Tim Rice
Music by Andrew Lloyd Webber

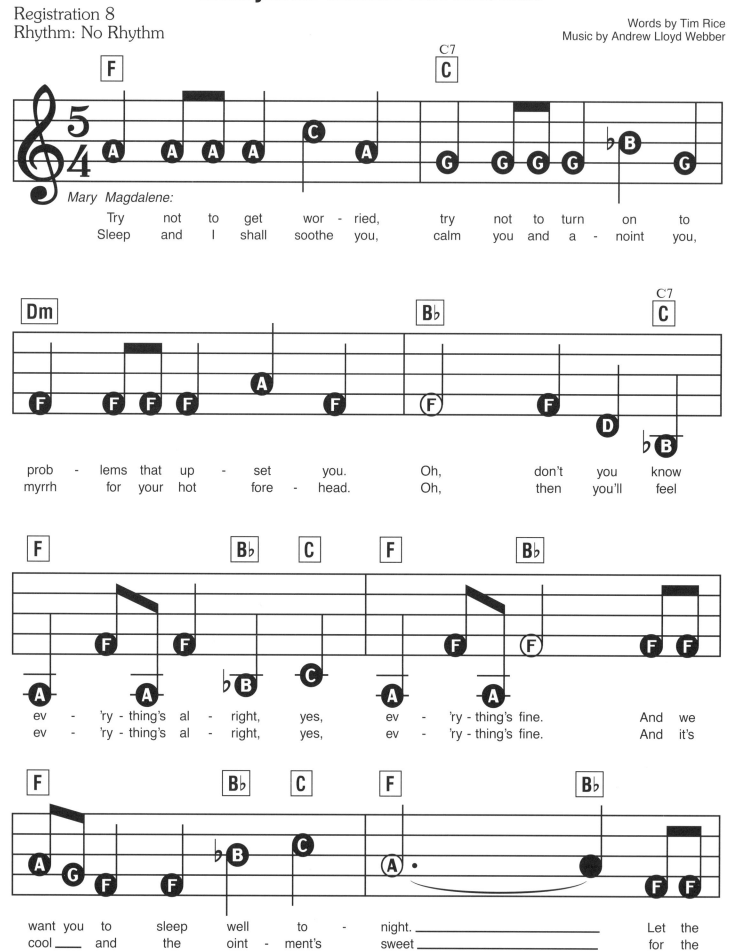

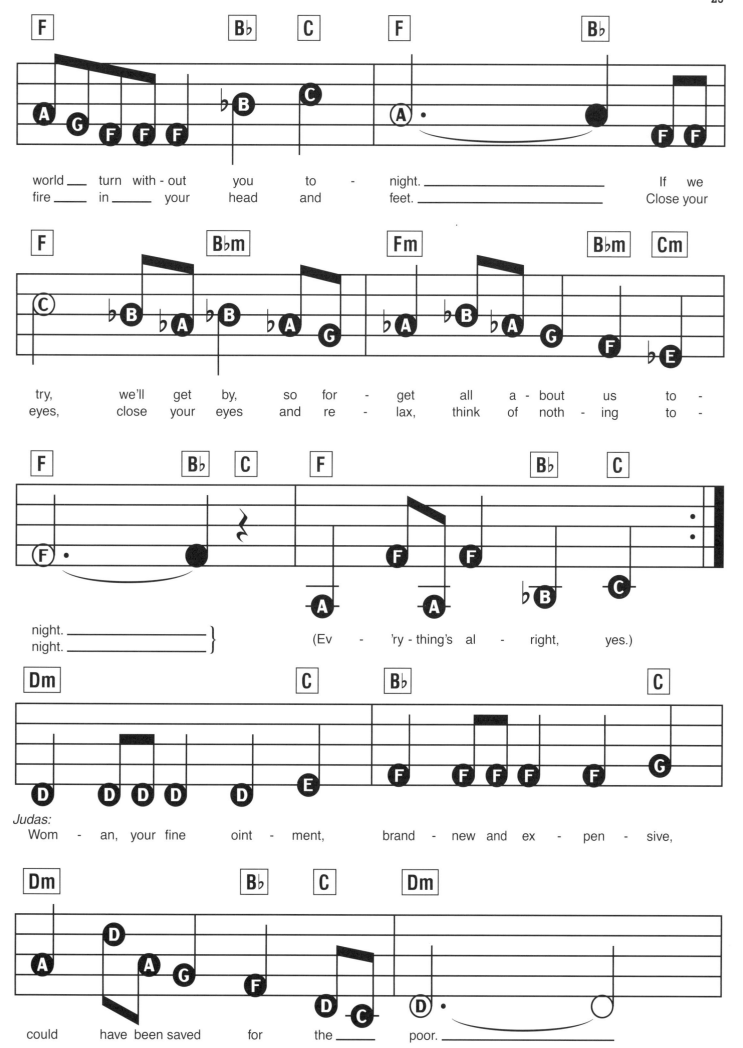

30

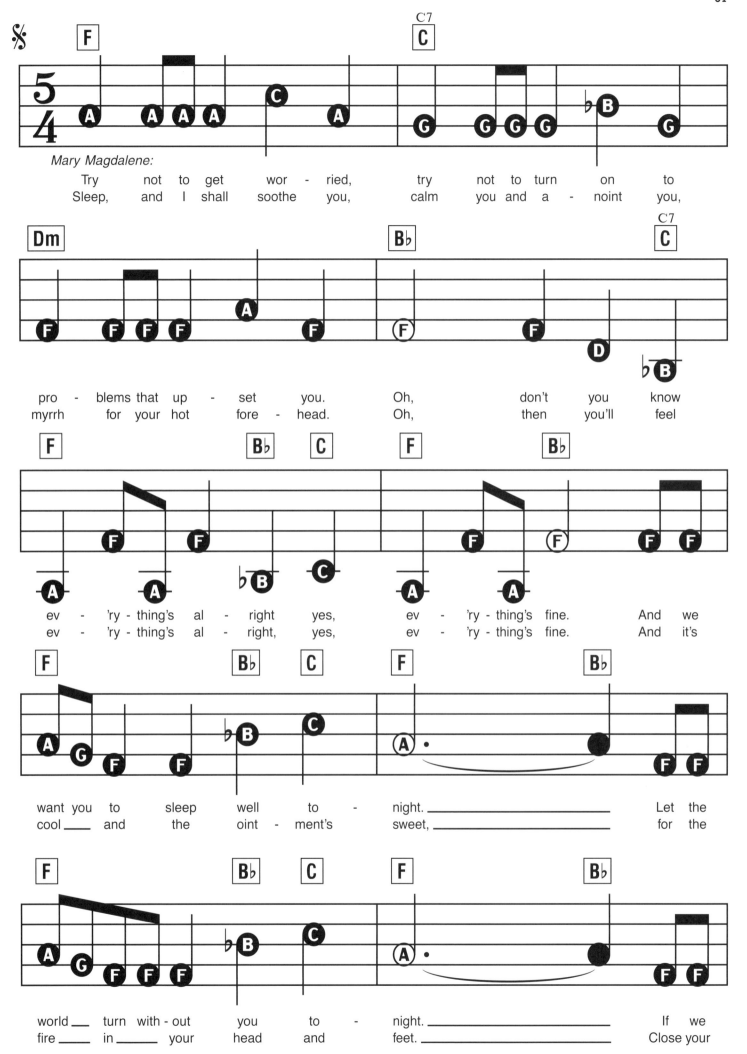

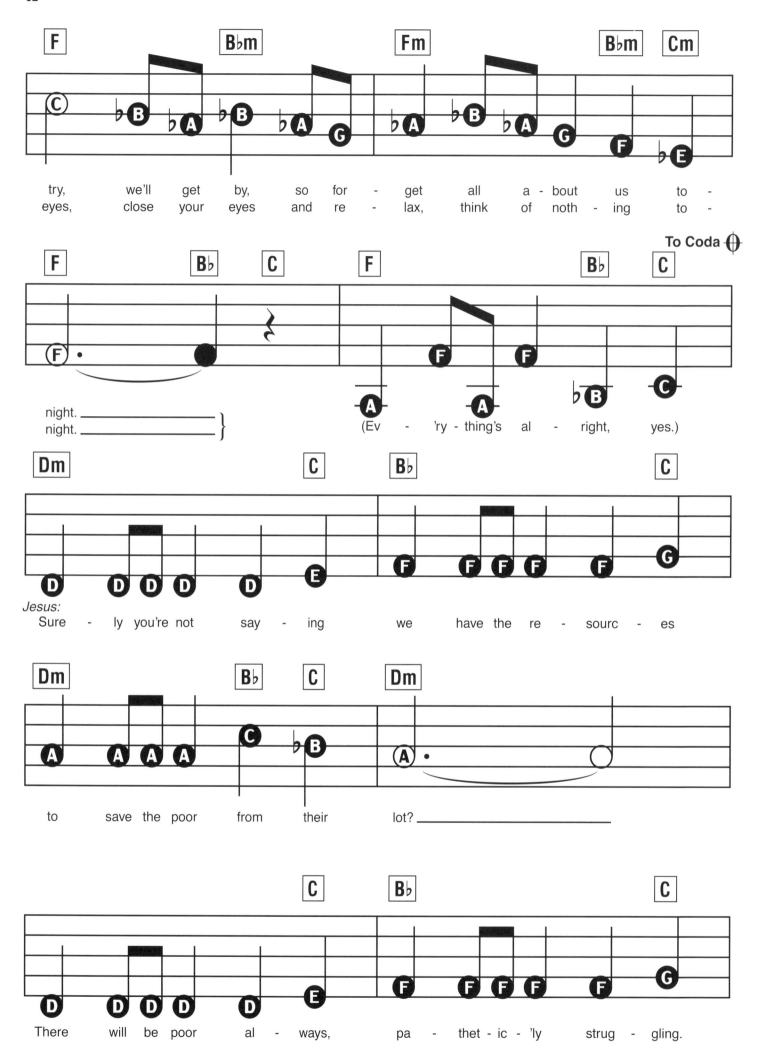

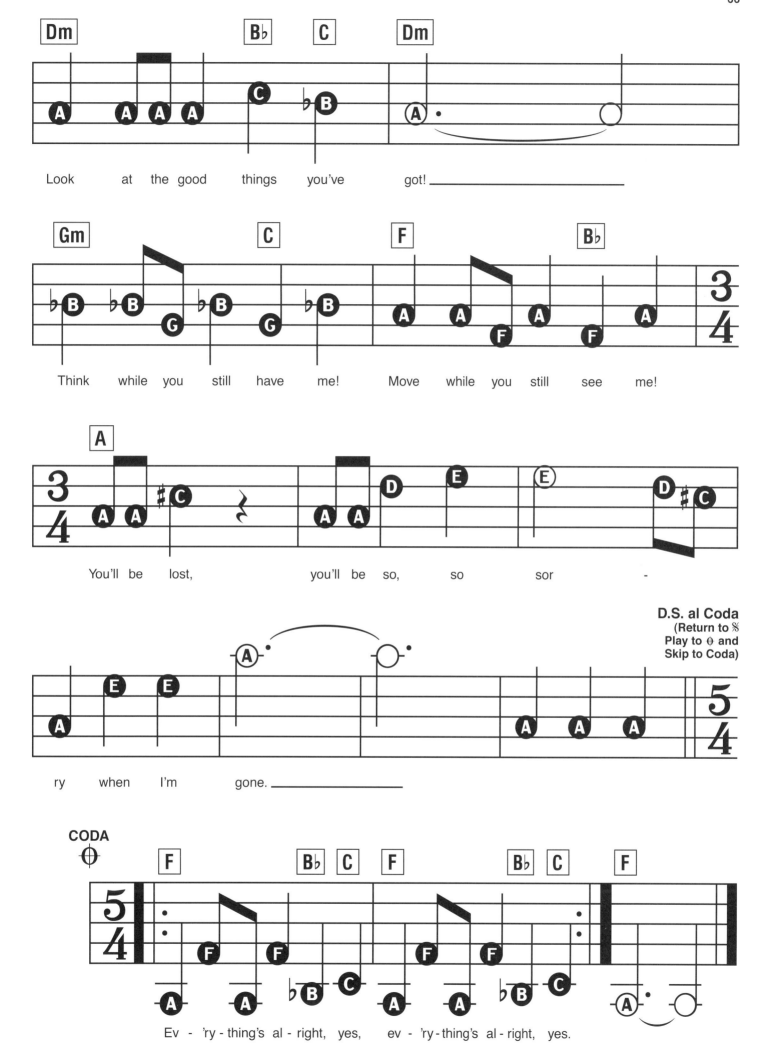

Look at the good things you've got!

Think while you still have me! Move while you still see me!

You'll be lost, you'll be so, so sor -

D.S. al Coda
(Return to 𝄋
Play to ⊕ and
Skip to Coda)

ry when I'm gone.

CODA

Ev - 'ry - thing's al - right, yes, ev - 'ry - thing's al - right, yes.

I Believe My Heart

from THE WOMAN IN WHITE

Registration 2
Rhythm: Ballad

Music by Andrew Lloyd Webber
Lyrics by David Zippel

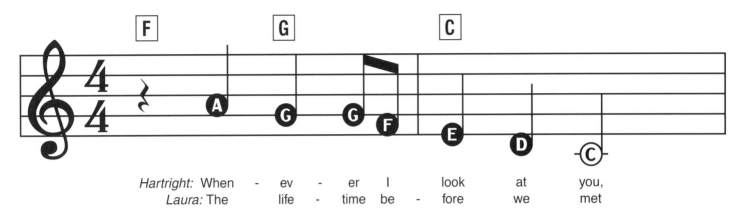

Hartright: When - ev - er I look at you,
Laura: The life - time be - fore we met

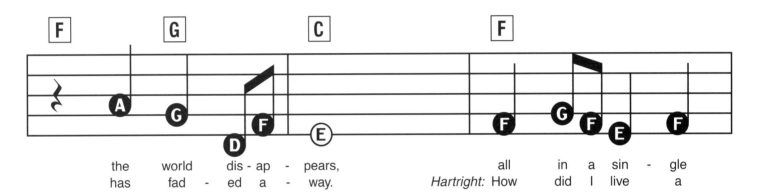

the world dis - ap - pears, all in a sin - gle
has fad - ed a - way. *Hartright:* How did I live a

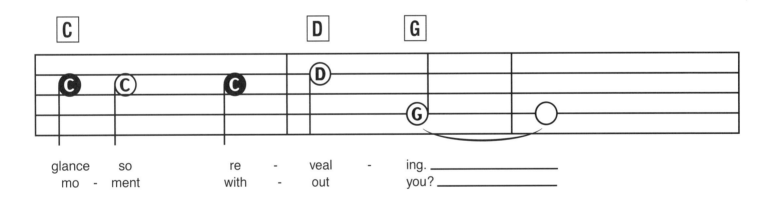

glance so re - veal - ing. _____
mo - ment with - out you? _____

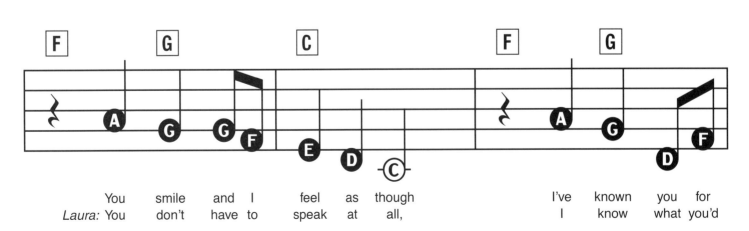

You smile and I feel as though I've known you for
Laura: You don't have to speak at all, I know what you'd

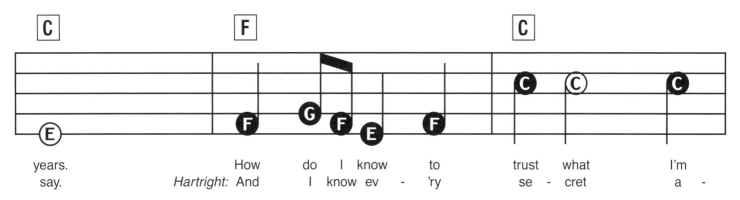

years.   How do I know to trust what I'm
say.   *Hartright:* And I know ev - 'ry se - cret a -

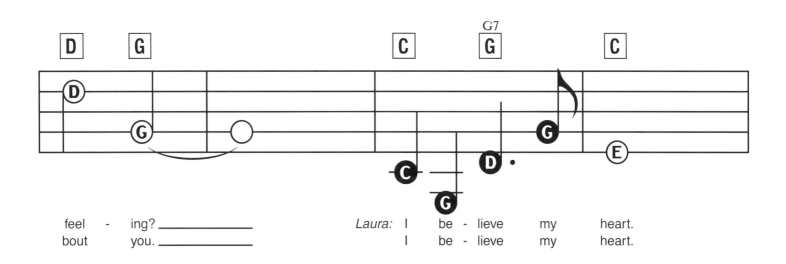

feel - ing? _____   *Laura:* I be - lieve my heart.
bout you. _____   I be - lieve my heart.

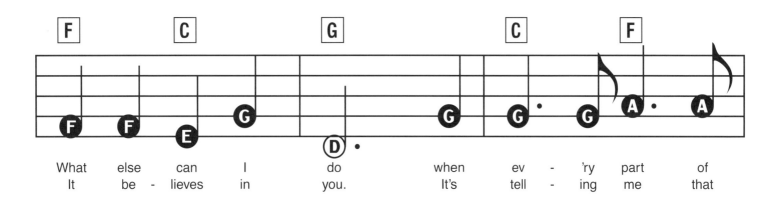

What else can I do when ev - 'ry part of
It be - lieves in you. It's tell - ing me that

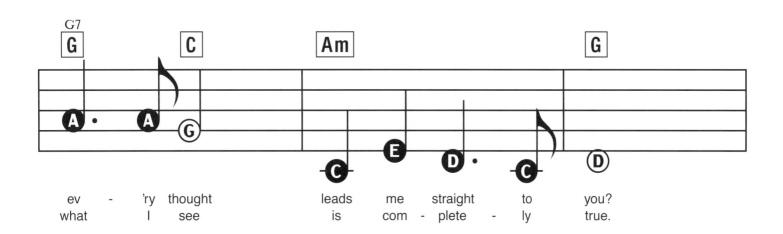

ev - 'ry thought leads me straight to you?
what I see is com - plete - ly true.

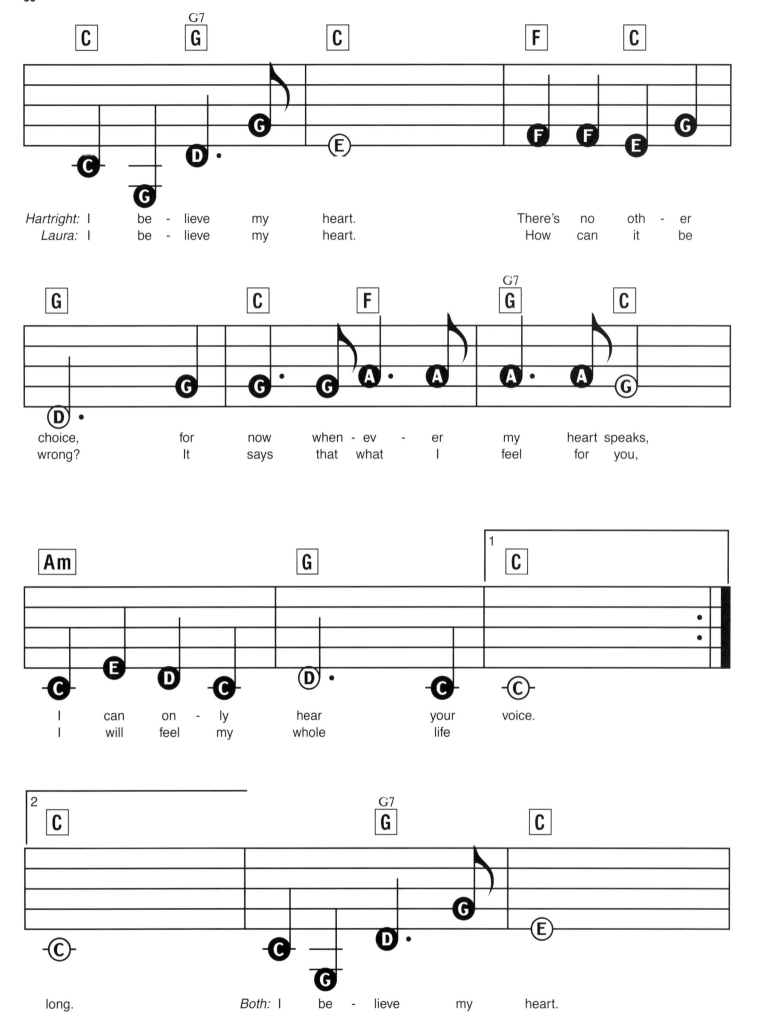

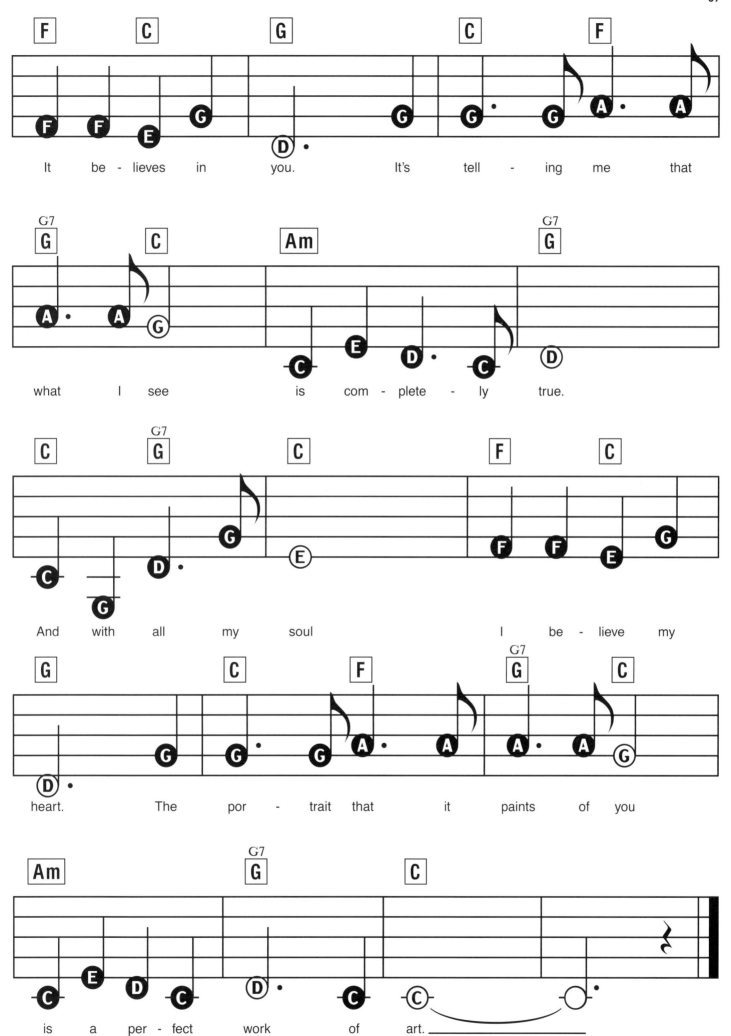

I Don't Know How to Love Him

from JESUS CHRIST SUPERSTAR

Registration 1
Rhythm: Ballad

Words by Tim Rice
Music by Andrew Lloyd Webber

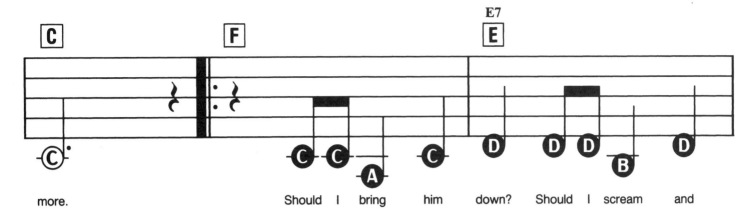

more. Should I bring him down? Should I scream and

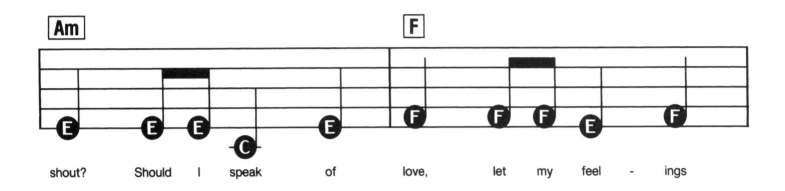

shout? Should I speak of love, let my feel - ings

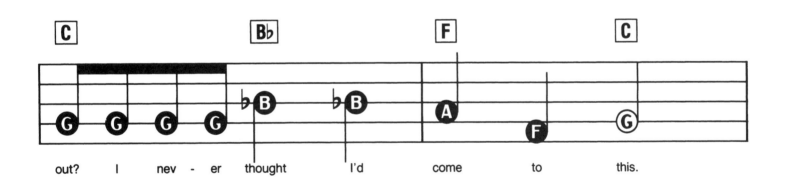

out? I nev - er thought I'd come to this.

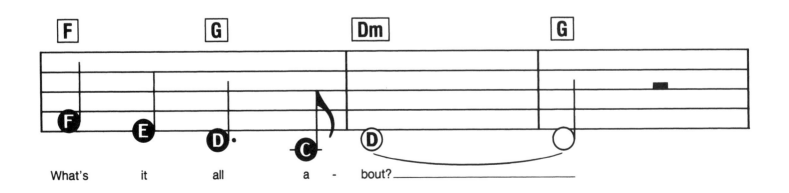

What's it all a - bout?

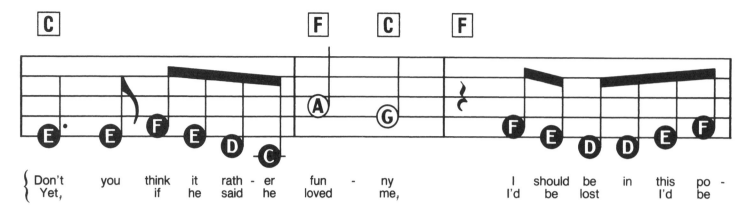

Don't you think it rath - er fun - ny
Yet, if he said he loved me,

I should be in this po -
I'd be lost I'd be

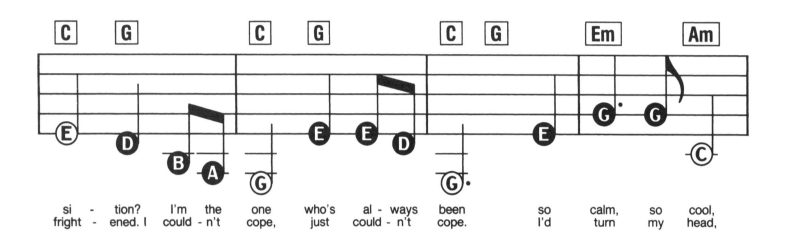

si - tion? I'm the one who's al - ways been
fright - ened. I could - n't cope, who's just could - n't cope.

so calm, so cool,
I'd turn my head,

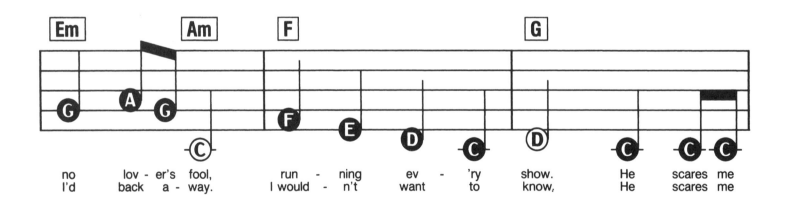

no lov - er's fool, run - ning ev - 'ry show.
I'd back a - way. I would - n't want to know,

He scares me
He scares me

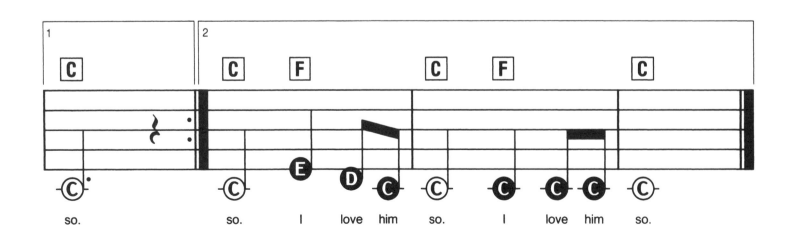

so.
so. I love him so. I love him so.

No Matter What
from WHISTLE DOWN THE WIND

Registration 1
Rhythm: 8 Beat or Ballad

Music by Andrew Lloyd Webber
Lyrics by Jim Steinman

No mat - ter what they   tell us,   no mat - ter what they
If on - ly tears were   laugh - ter,   if on - ly night was

do,   no mat - ter what they   teach us,   what we be - lieve is
day,   if on - ly prayers were   an - swered,   then we would hear God

true.   No mat - ter what they   call   us,
say: No mat - ter what they   tell   you,

how - ev - er they at - tack,   no mat - ter where they take us,
no mat - ter what they do,   no mat - ter what they teach you,

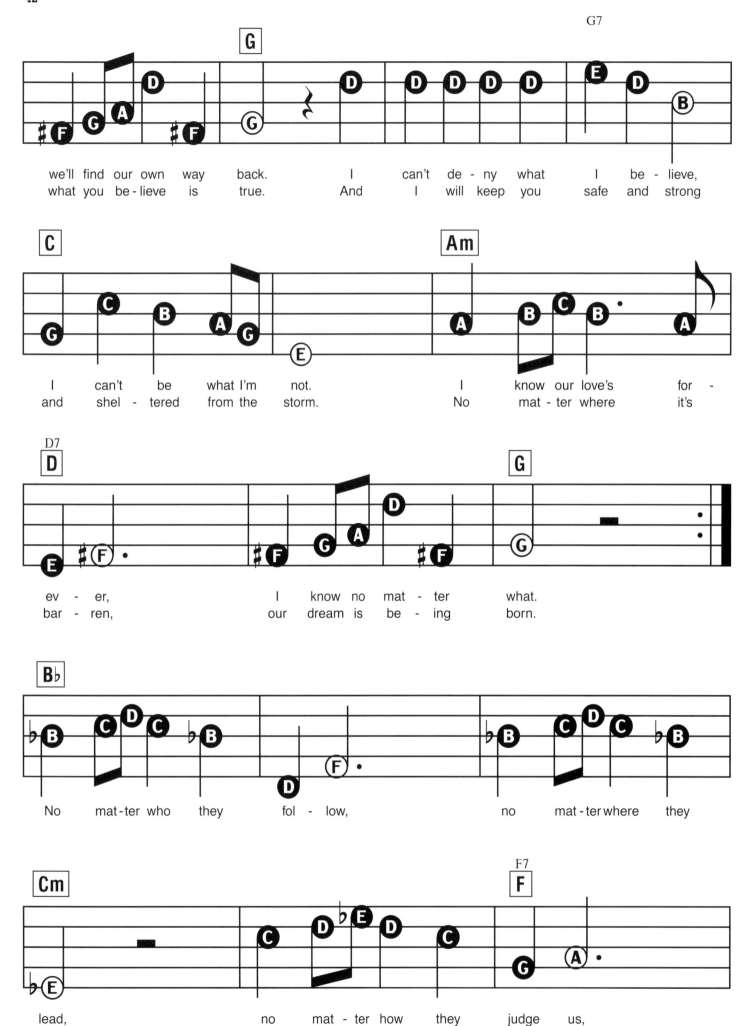

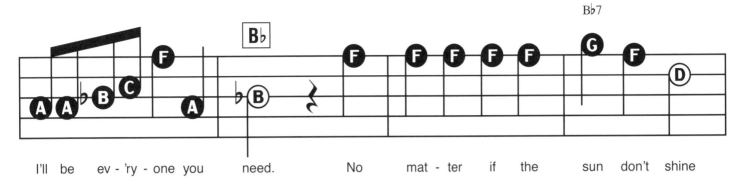

I'll be ev - 'ry-one you need. No mat - ter if the sun don't shine

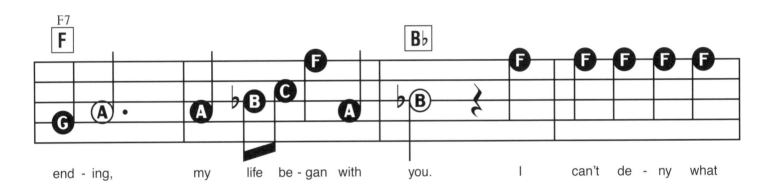

or if the skies are blue, no mat - ter what the

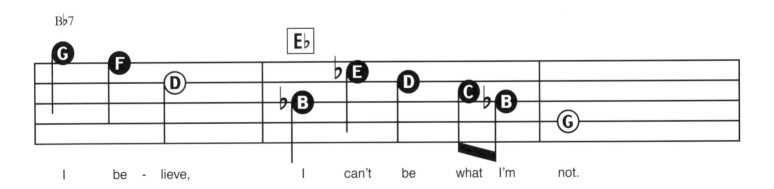

end - ing, my life be - gan with you. I can't de - ny what

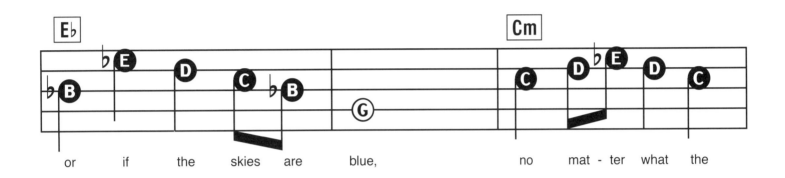

I be - lieve, I can't be what I'm not.

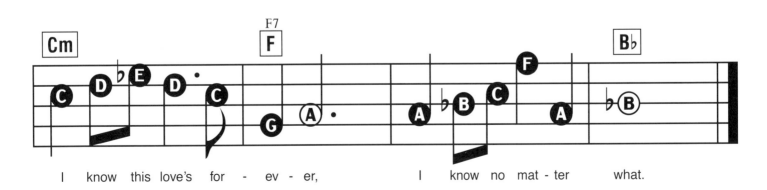

I know this love's for - ev - er, I know no mat - ter what.

I'm Hopeless When It Comes to You
from STEPHEN WARD

Registration 2
Rhythm: 4/4 Ballad

Music by Andrew Lloyd Webber
Book and Lyrics by Don Black and Christopher Hampton

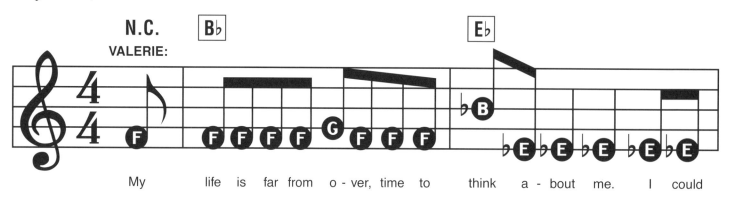

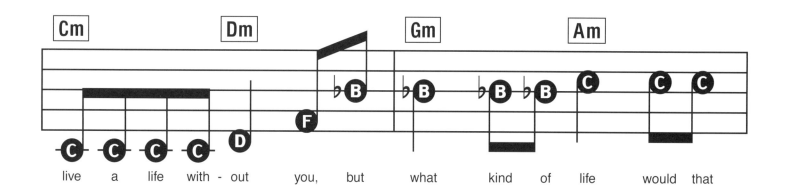

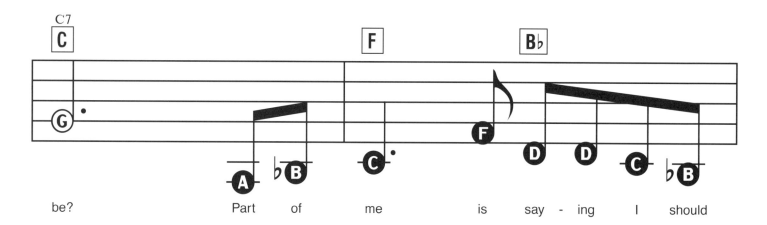

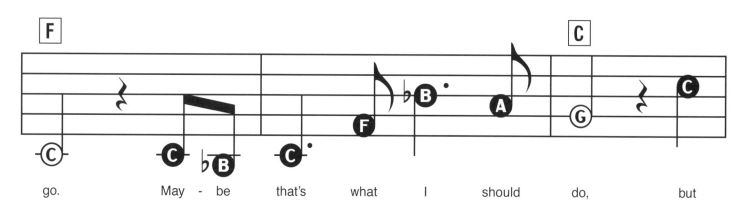

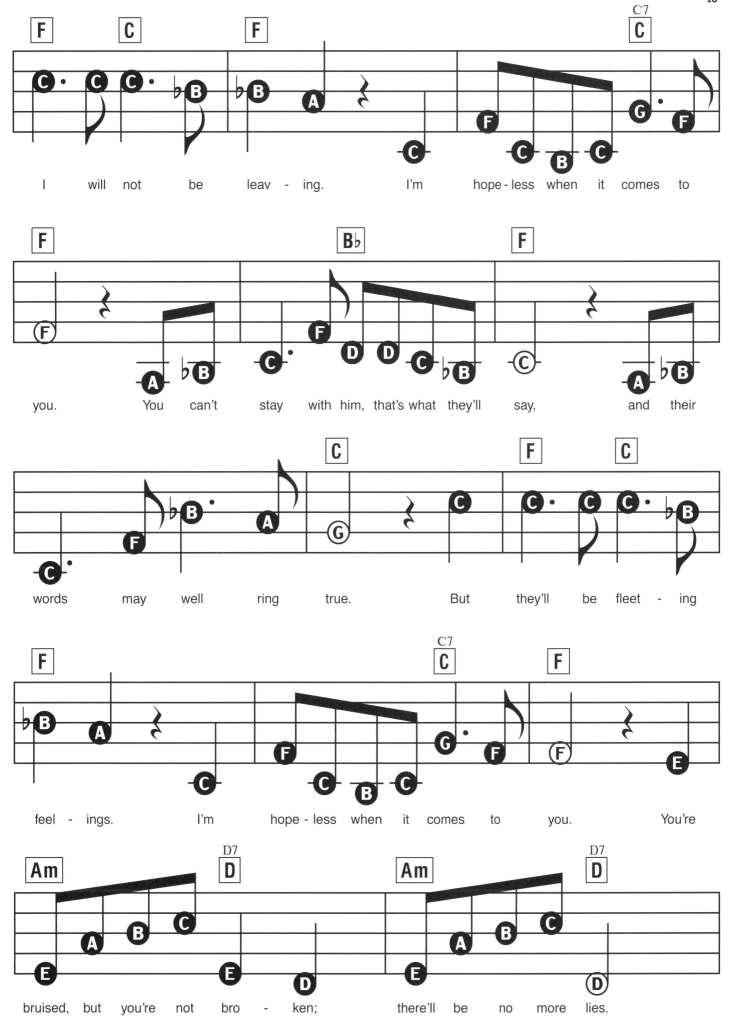

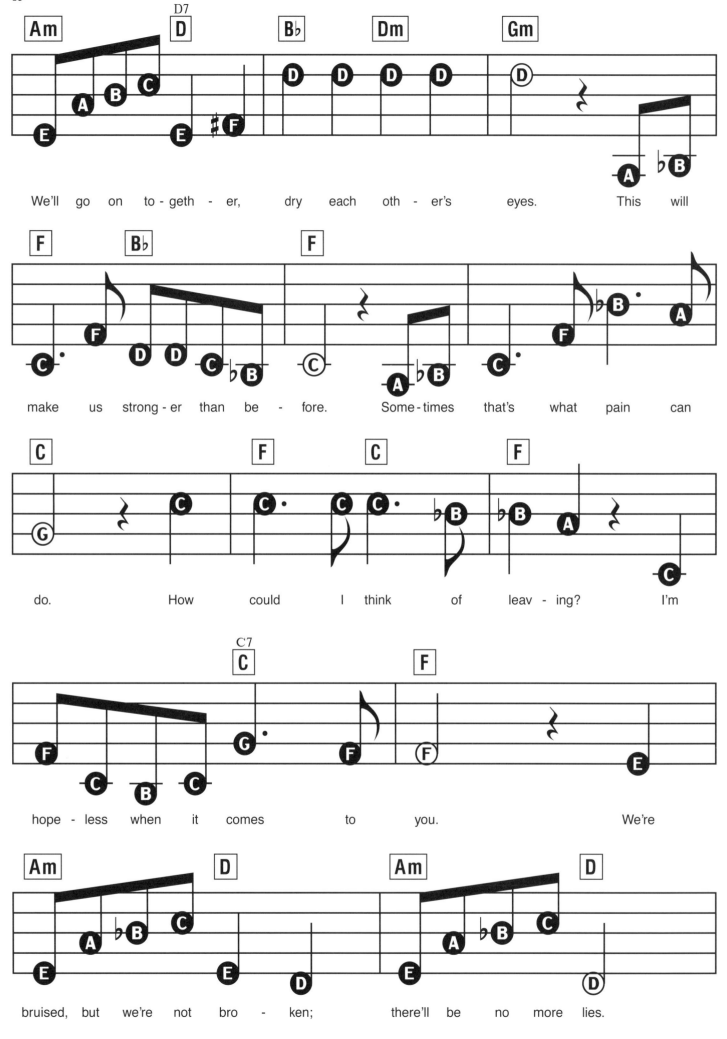

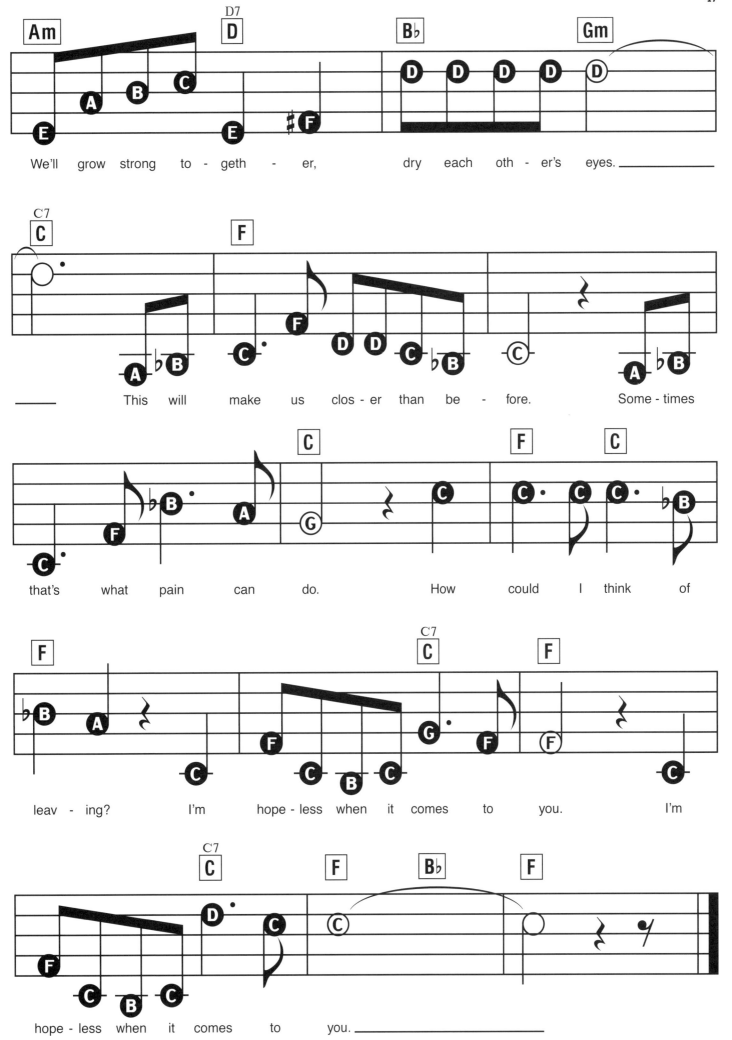

Love Changes Everything
from ASPECTS OF LOVE

Registration 2
Rhythm: Rock or 8-Beat

Music by Andrew Lloyd Webber
Lyrics by Don Black and Charles Hart

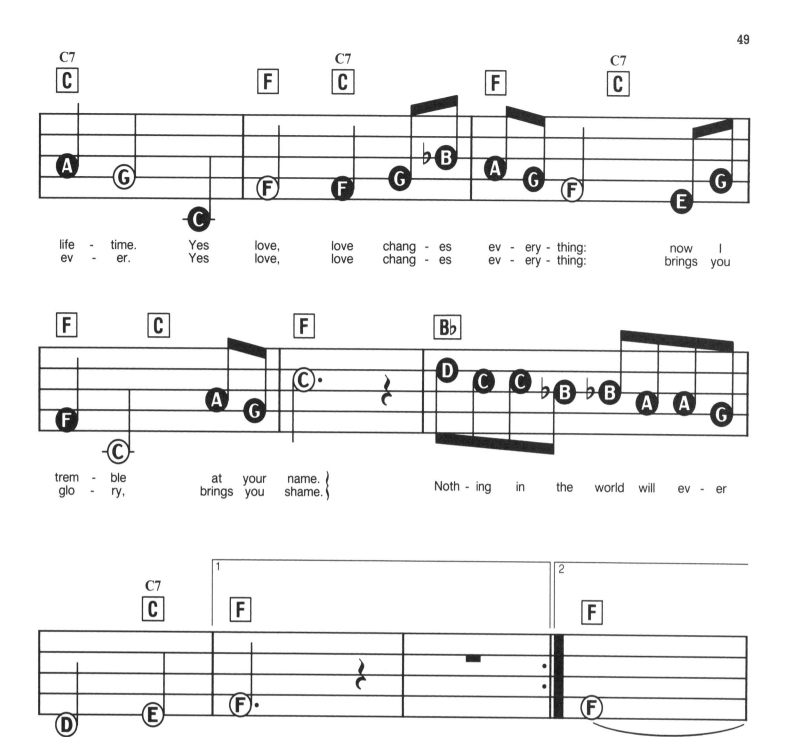

life - time. Yes love, love chang - es ev - ery - thing: now I
ev - er. Yes love, love chang - es ev - ery - thing: brings you

trem - ble at your name. }
glo - ry, brings you shame. }

Noth - ing in the world will ev - er

be the same.

same.

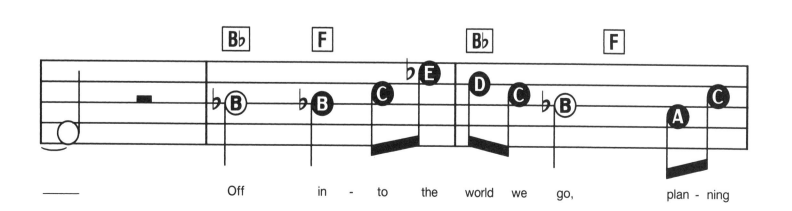

Off in - to the world we go, plan - ning

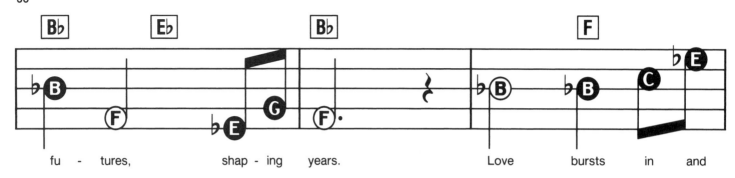

fu - tures, shap - ing years. Love bursts in and

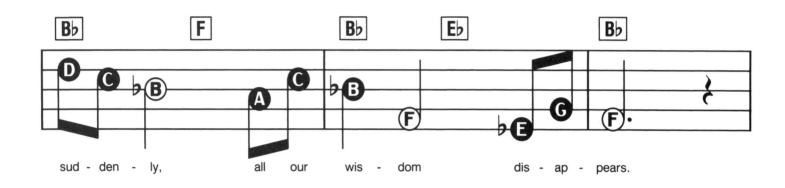

sud - den - ly, all our wis - dom dis - ap - pears.

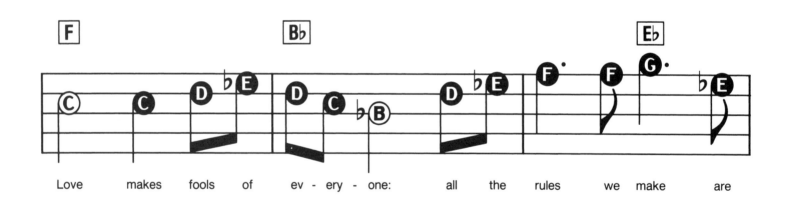

Love makes fools of ev - ery - one: all the rules we make are

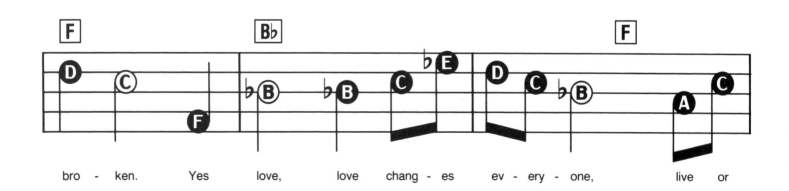

bro - ken. Yes love, love chang - es ev - ery - one, live or

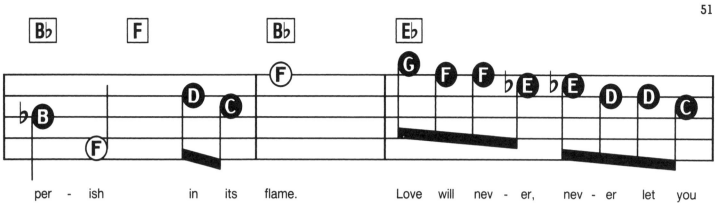

per - ish in its flame. Love will nev - er, nev - er let you

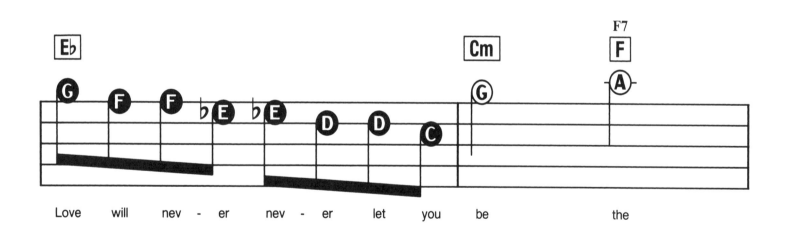

be the same.

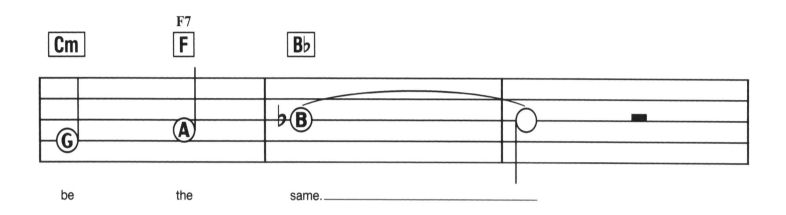

Love will nev - er nev - er let you be the

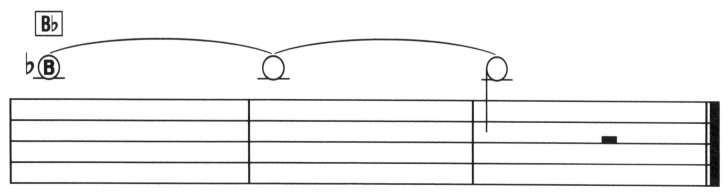

same.

Love Never Dies
from LOVE NEVER DIES

Registration 8
Rhythm: None

Music by Andrew Lloyd Webber
Lyrics by Glenn Slater

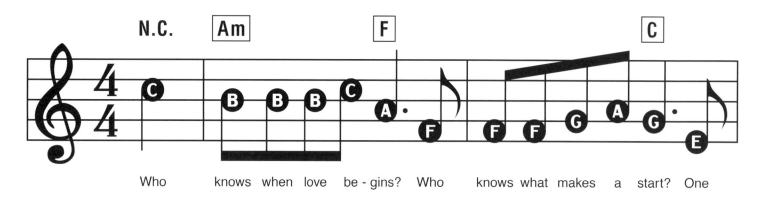

Who knows when love be - gins? Who knows what makes a start? One

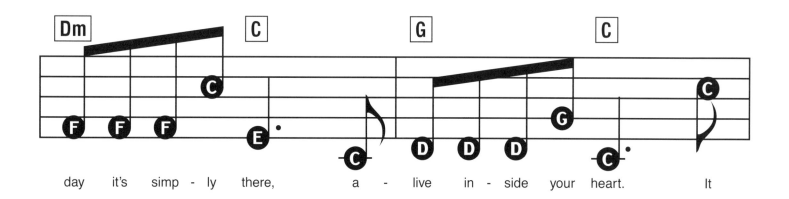

day it's simp - ly there, a - live in - side your heart. It

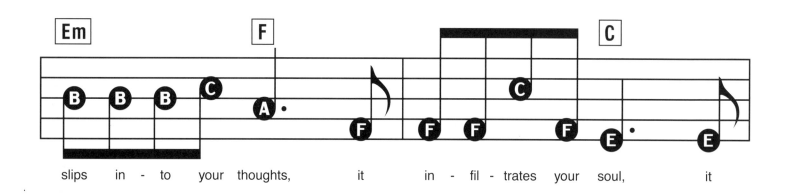

slips in - to your thoughts, it in - fil - trates your soul, it

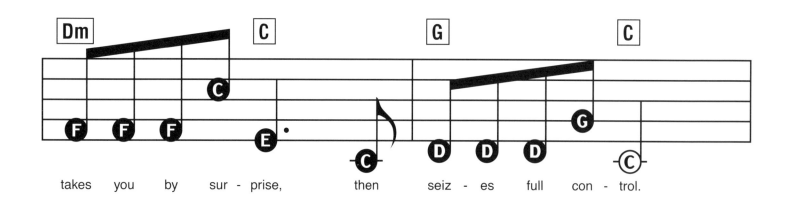

takes you by sur - prise, then seiz - es full con - trol.

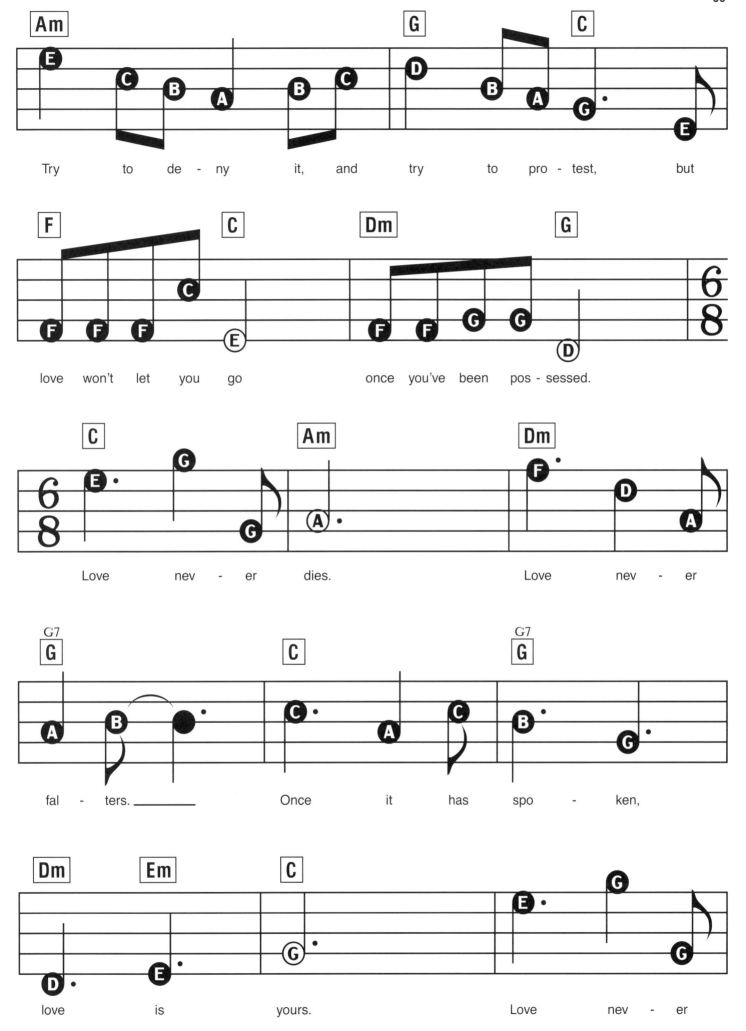

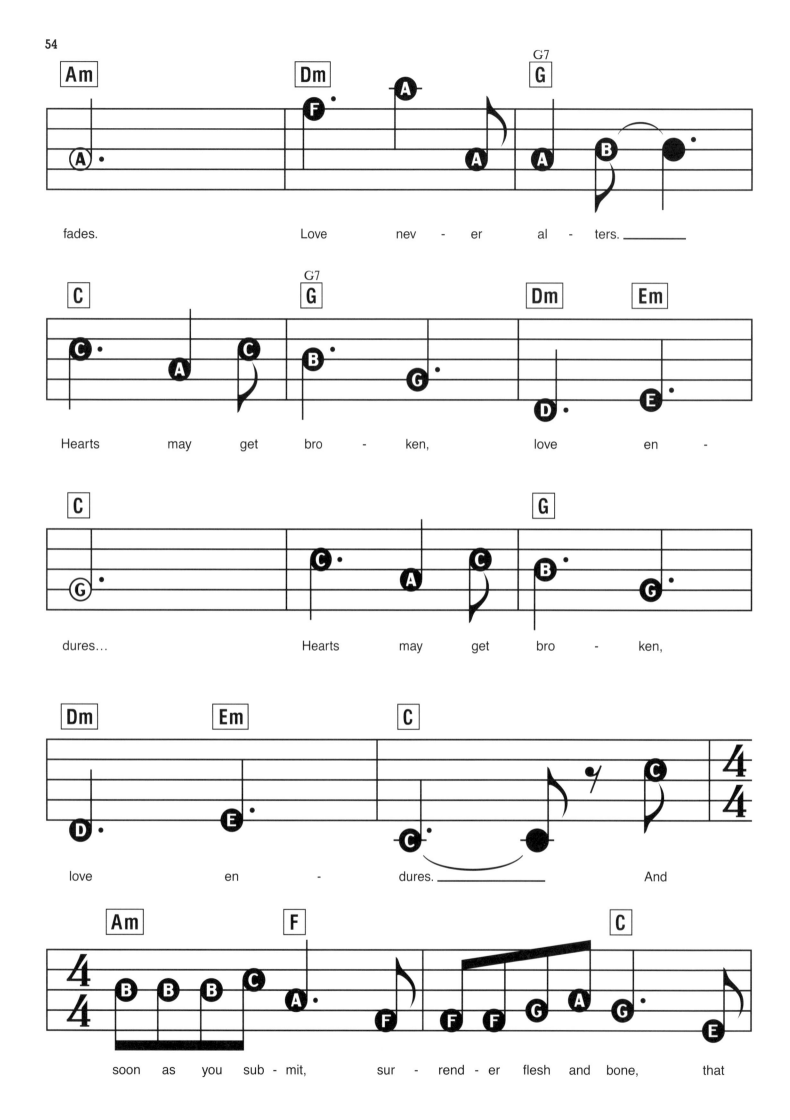

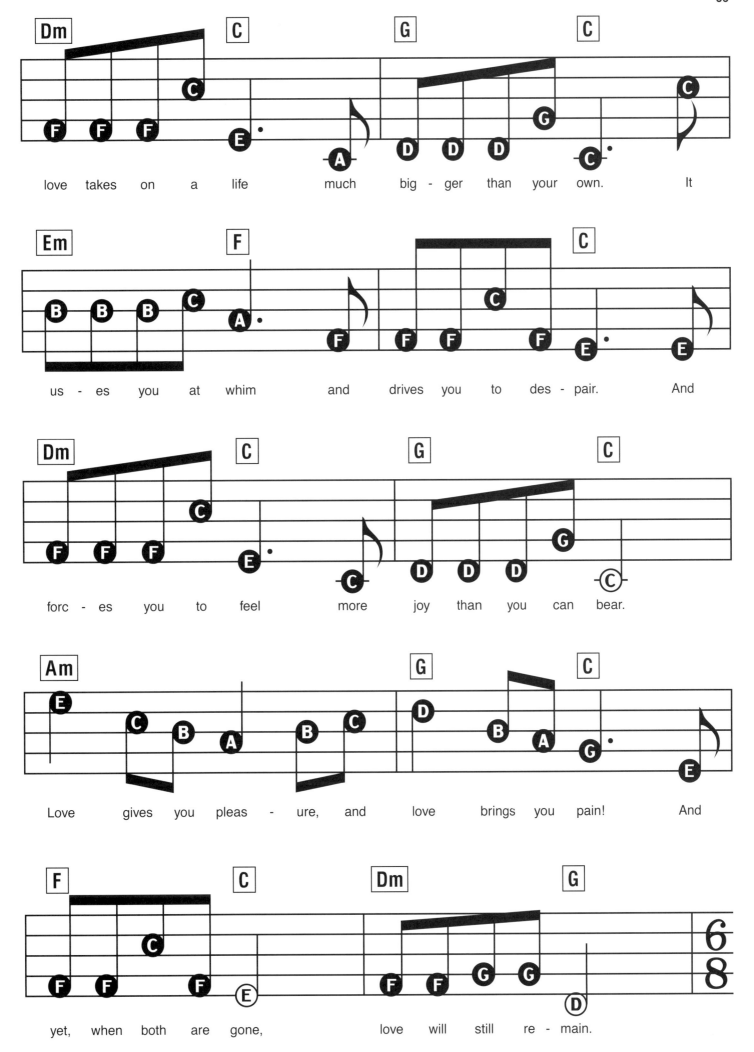

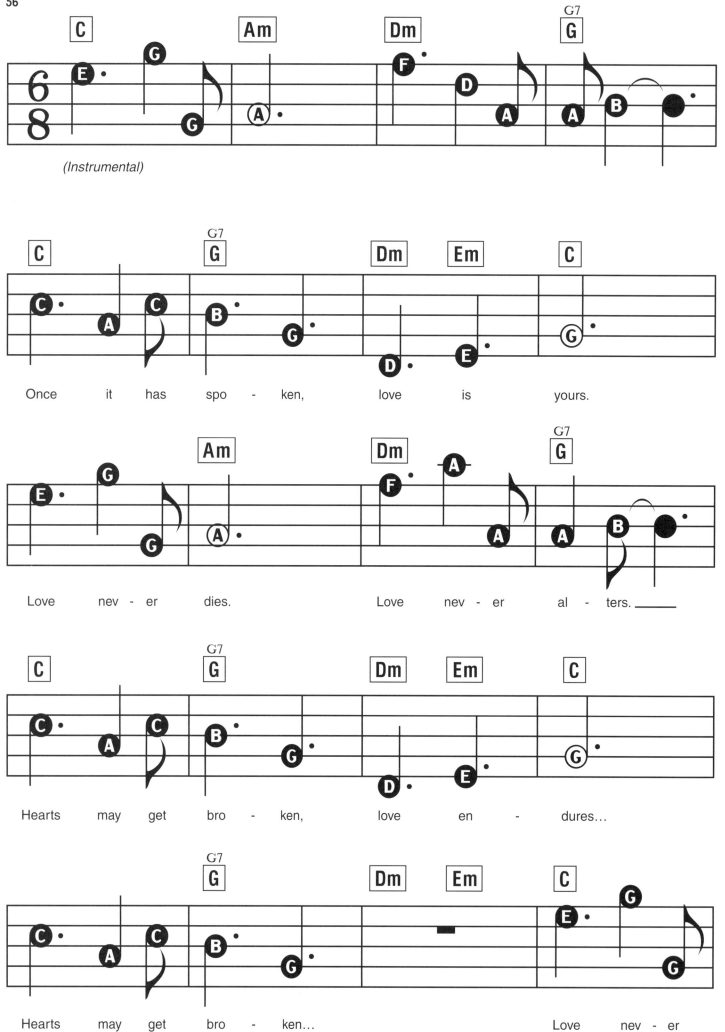

(Instrumental)

Once it has spo - ken, love is yours.

Love nev - er dies. Love nev - er al - ters. _____

Hearts may get bro - ken, love en - dures…

Hearts may get bro - ken… Love nev - er

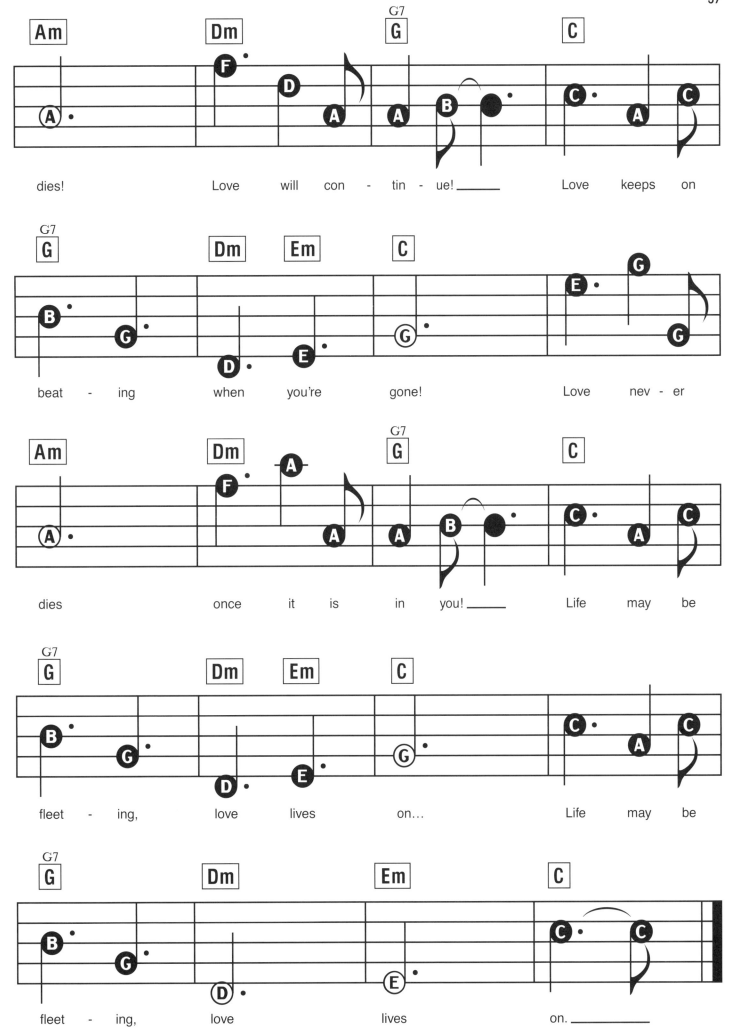

Memory
from CATS

Registration 3
Rhythm: 6/8 March

Music by Andrew Lloyd Webber
Text by Trevor Nunn after T.S. Eliot

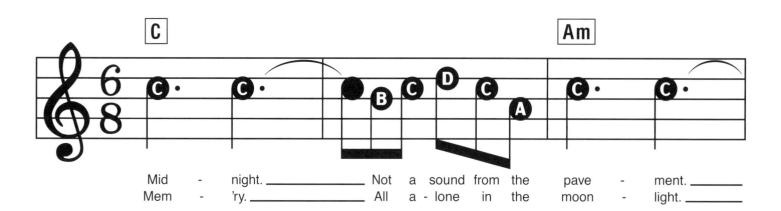

Mid - night. _____ Not a sound from the pave - ment. _____
Mem - 'ry. _____ All a - lone in the moon - light. _____

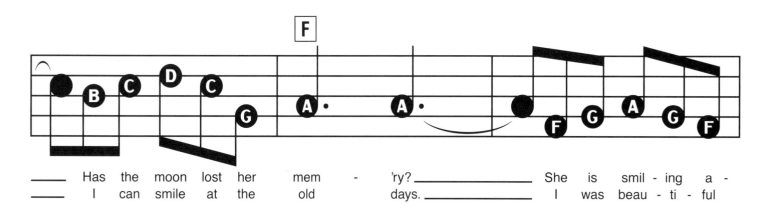

_____ Has the moon lost her mem - 'ry? _____ She is smil - ing a -
_____ I can smile at the old days. _____ I was beau - ti - ful

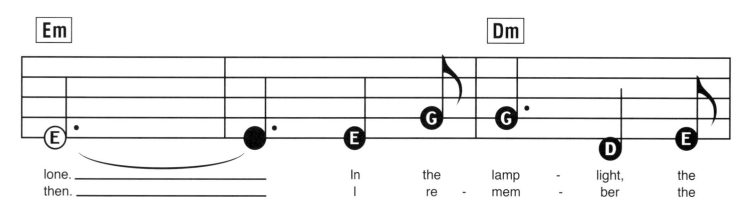

lone. _____ In the lamp - light, the
then. _____ I re - mem - ber the

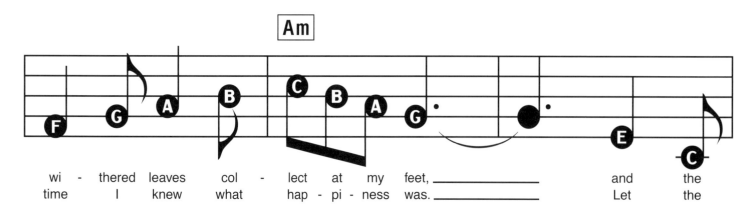

wi - thered leaves col - lect at my feet, _____ and the
time I knew what hap - pi - ness was. _____ Let the

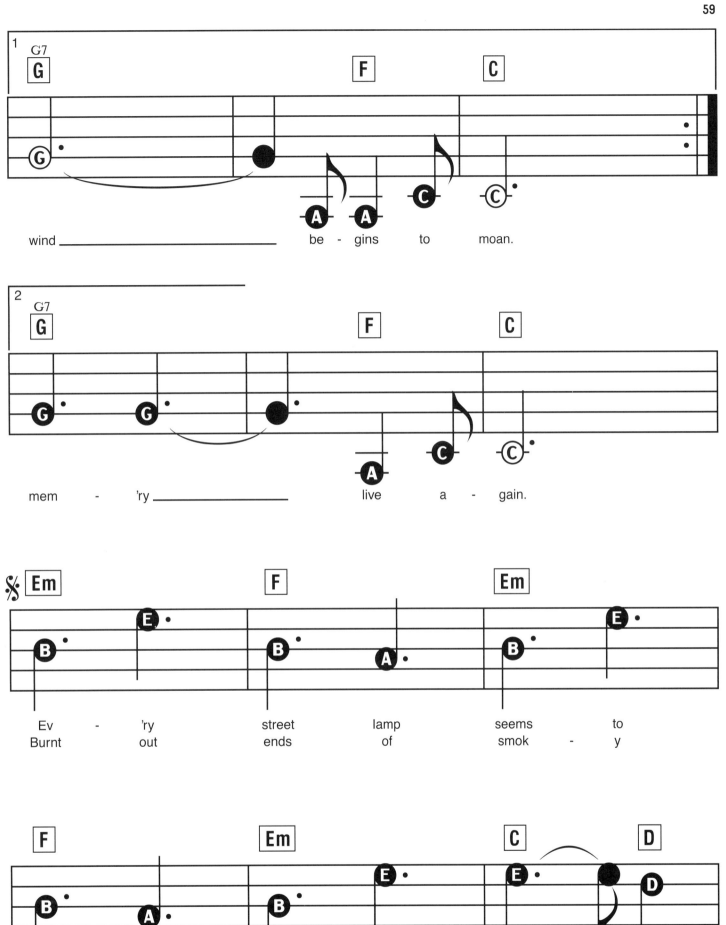

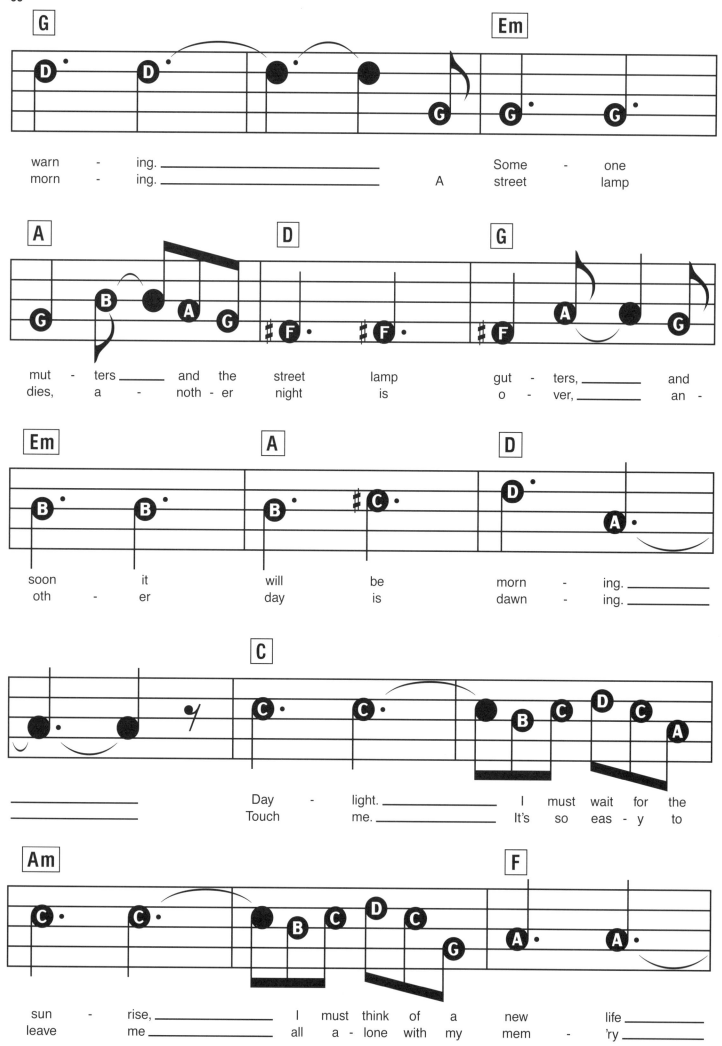

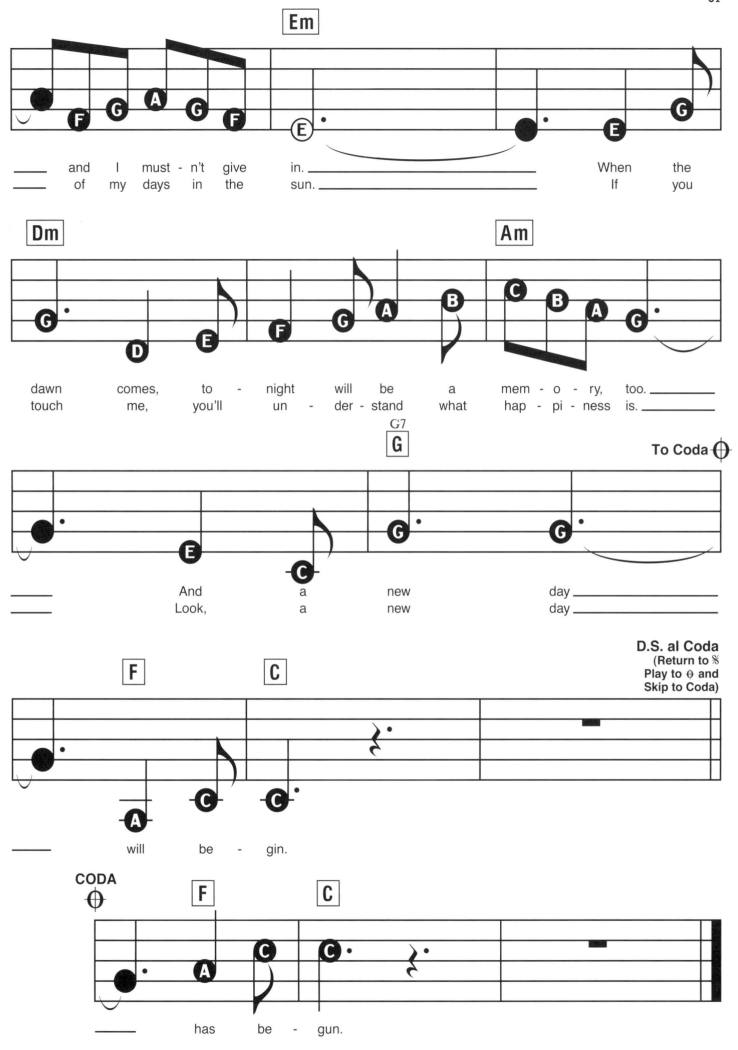

The Music of the Night
from THE PHANTOM OF THE OPERA

Registration 10
Rhythm: Ballad

Music by Andrew Lloyd Webber
Lyrics by Charles Hart
Additional Lyrics by Richard Stilgoe

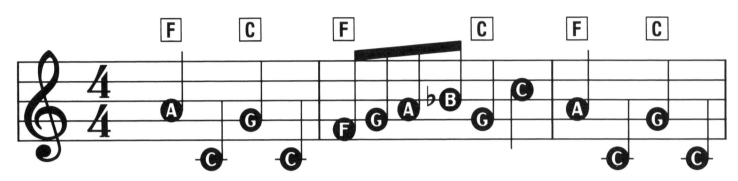

Phantom: Night - time sharp - ens, height- ens each sen - sa - tion; dark - ness stirs and

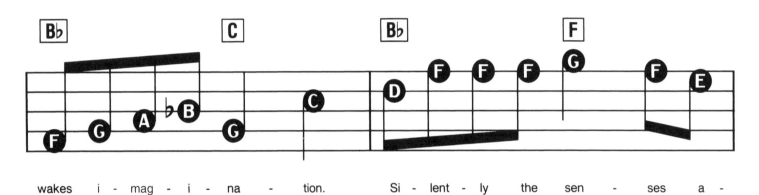

wakes i - mag - i - na - tion. Si - lent - ly the sen - ses a -

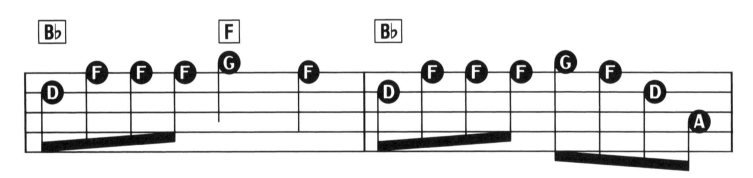

ban - don their de - fen - ses. *(Instrumental)*

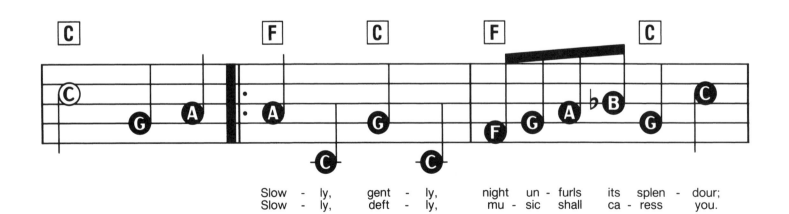

Slow - ly, gent - ly, night un - furls its splen - dour;
Slow - ly, deft - ly, mu - sic shall ca - ress you.

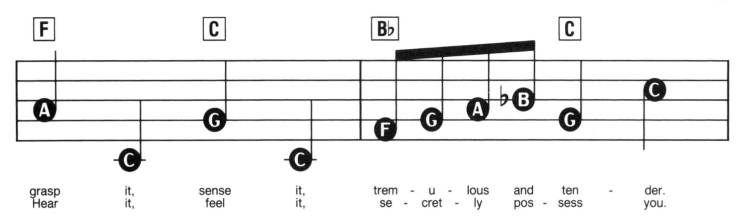

grasp   it,   sense   it,   trem - u - lous and ten - der.
Hear   it,   feel   it,   se - cret - ly pos - sess you.

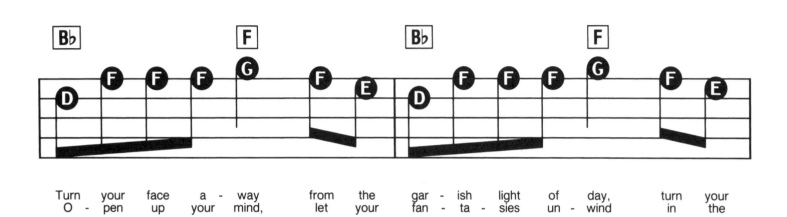

Turn your face a - way from the gar - ish light of day, turn your
O - pen up your mind, let your fan - ta - sies un - wind turn in the

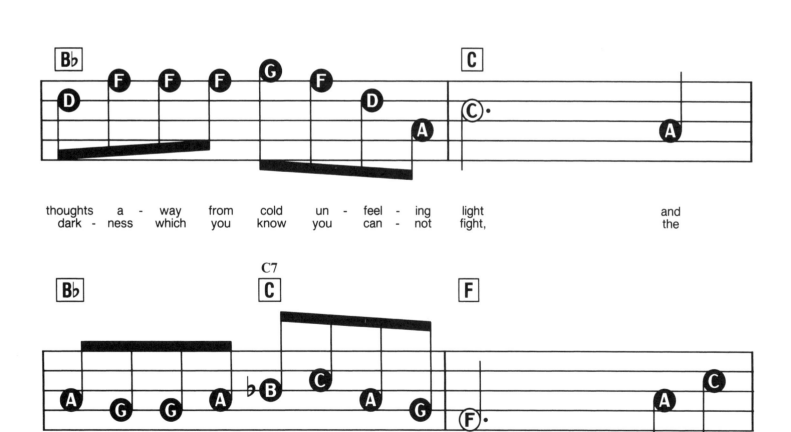

thoughts a - way from cold un - feel - ing light and
dark - ness which you know you can - not fight, the

lis - ten to the mu - sic of the night. Close your
dark - ness of the mu - sic of the night. Let your

64

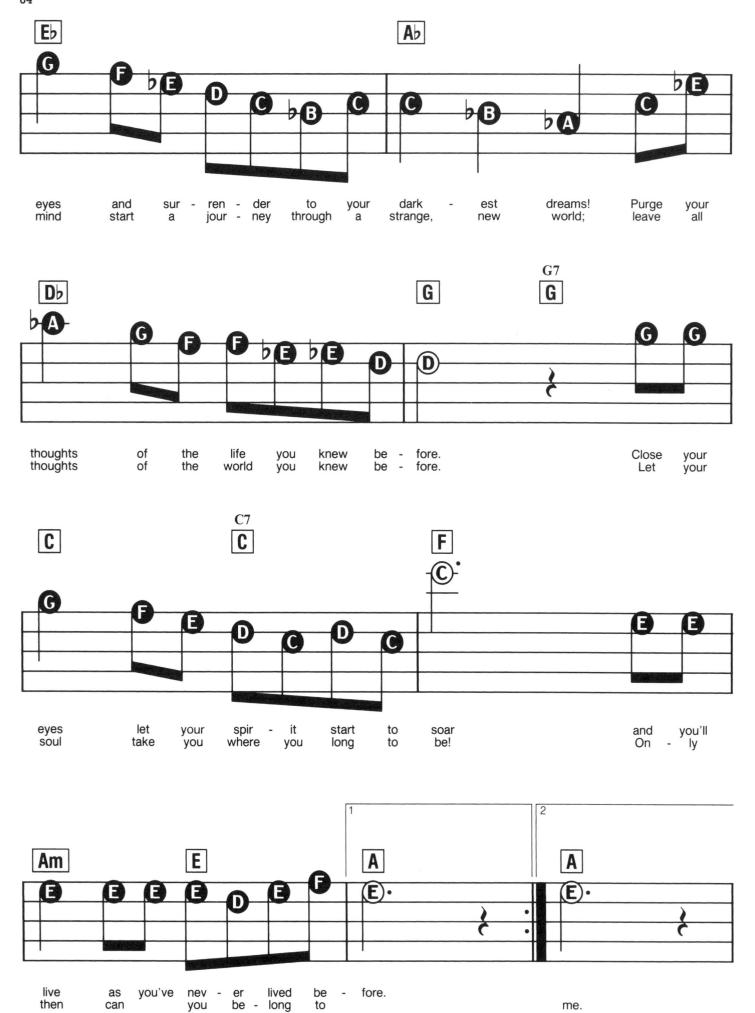

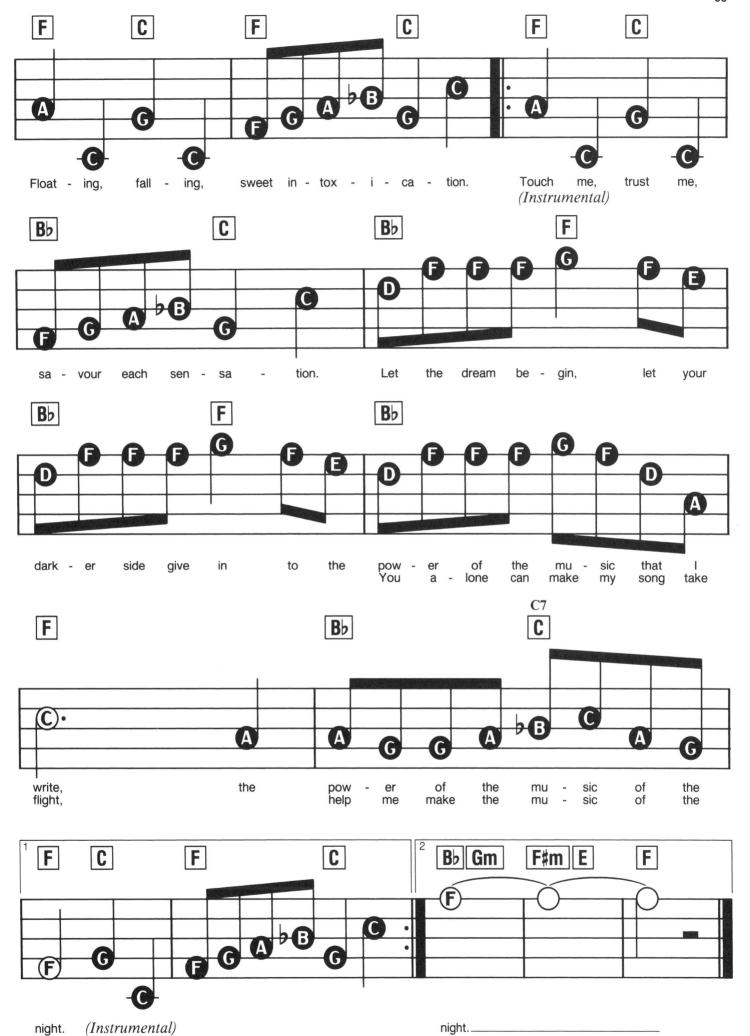

The Perfect Year
from SUNSET BOULEVARD

Registration 3
Rhythm: None

Music by Andrew Lloyd Webber
Lyrics by Don Black and Christopher Hampton

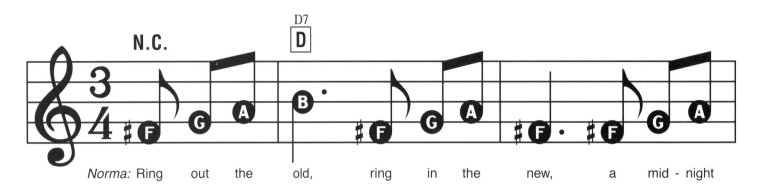

Norma: Ring out the old, ring in the new, a mid - night

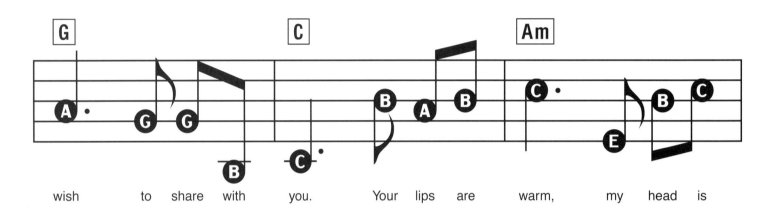

wish to share with you. Your lips are warm, my head is

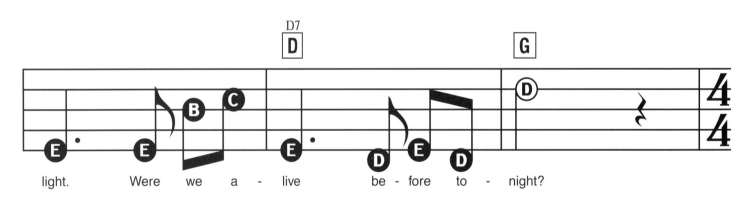

light. Were we a - live be - fore to - night?

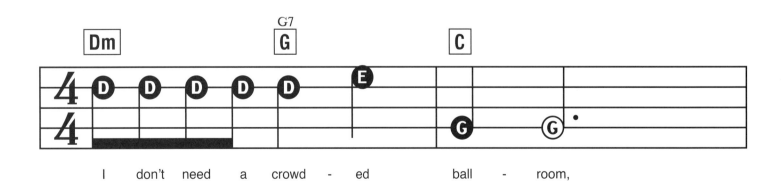

I don't need a crowd - ed ball - room,

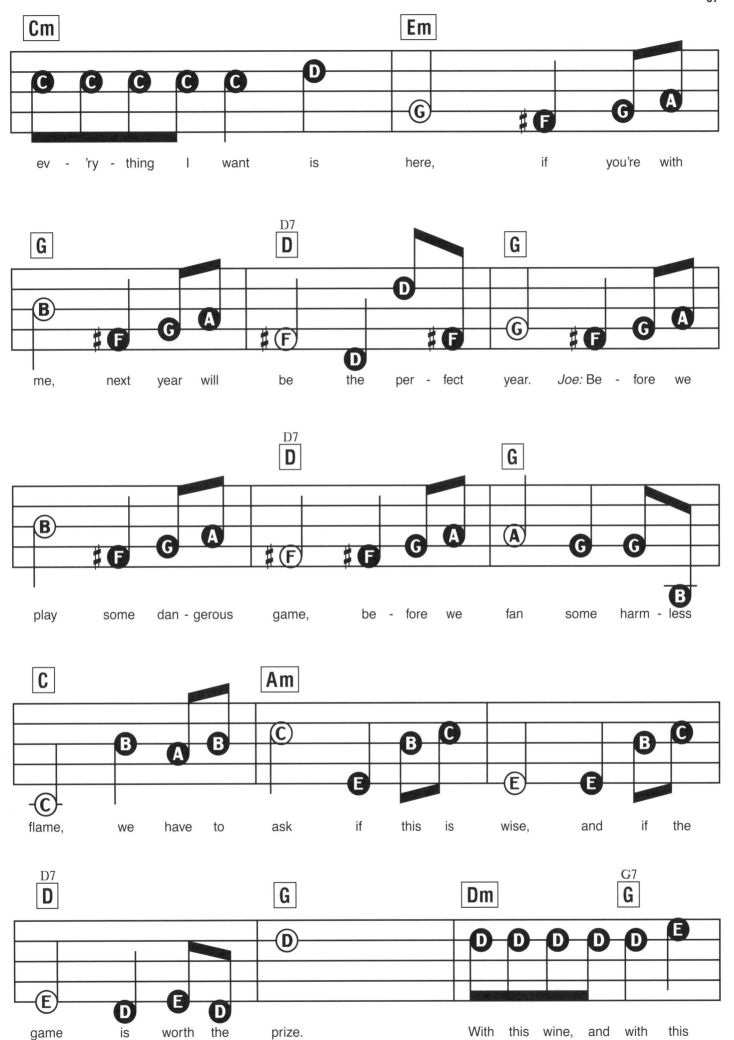

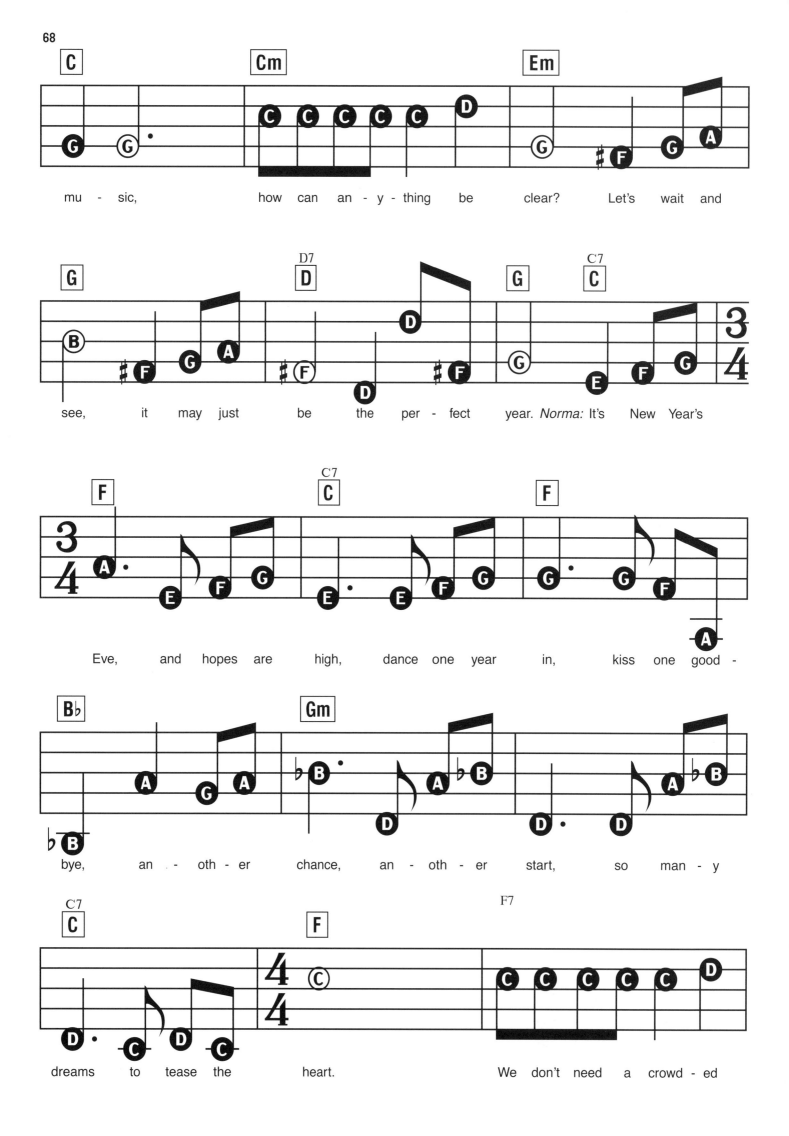

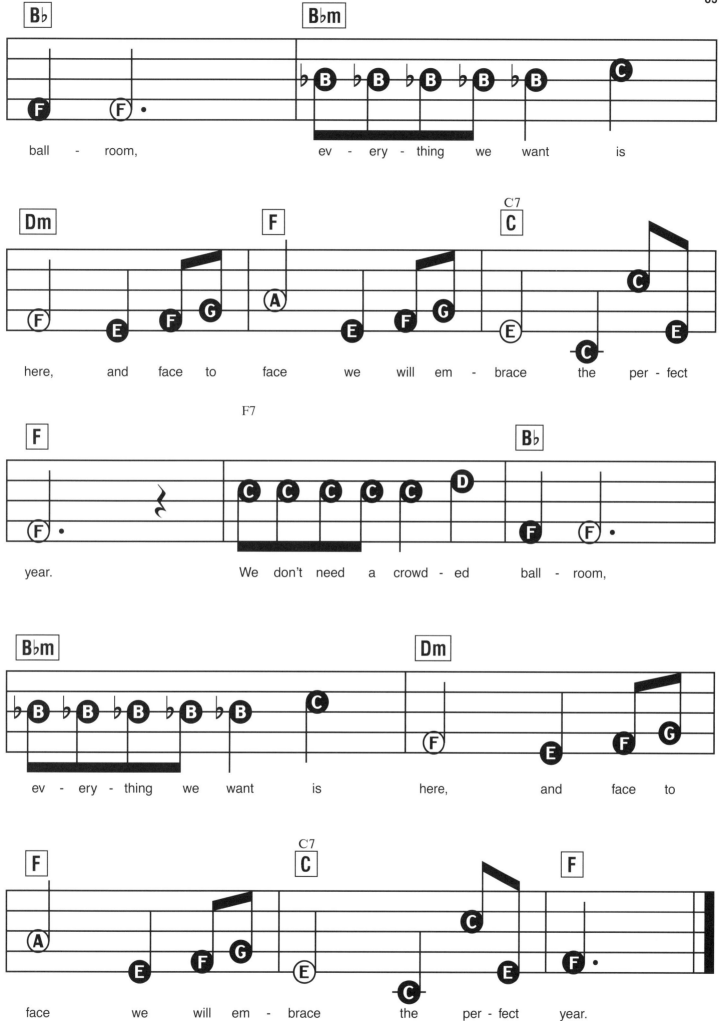

The Phantom of the Opera
from The PHANTOM OF THE OPERA

Music by Andrew Lloyd Webber
Lyrics by Charles Hart
Additional Lyrics by Richard Stilgoe and Mike Batt

Registration 6
Rhythm: Disco, 8-Beat, or Rock

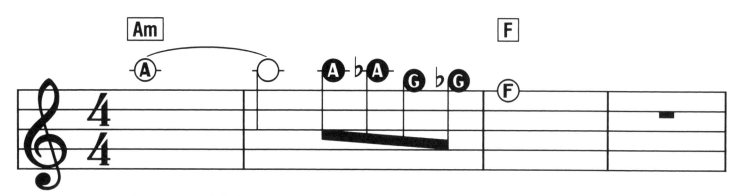

(Instrumental Solo)

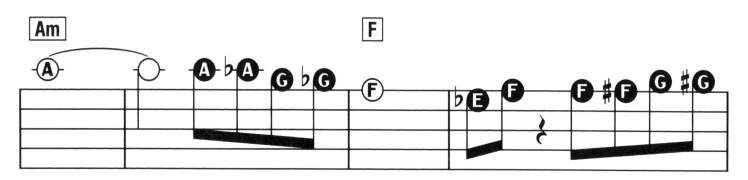

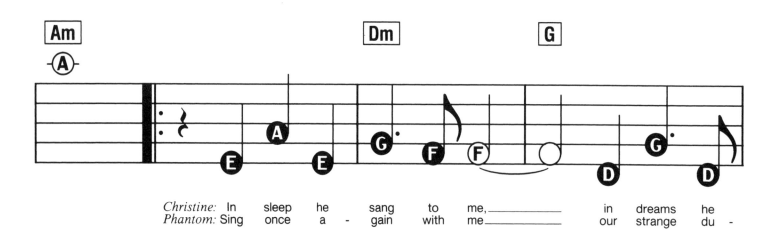

Christine: In sleep he sang to me,_____ in dreams he
Phantom: Sing once a - gain with me_____ our strange du -

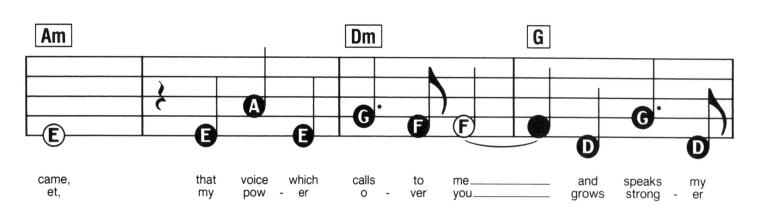

came, that voice which calls to me_____ and speaks my
et, my pow - er o - ver you_____ grows strong - er

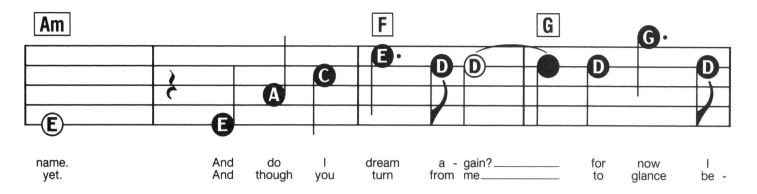

name.   And   do   I   dream   a - gain?_____   for   now   I
yet.   And though   you   turn   from me_____   to   glance be -

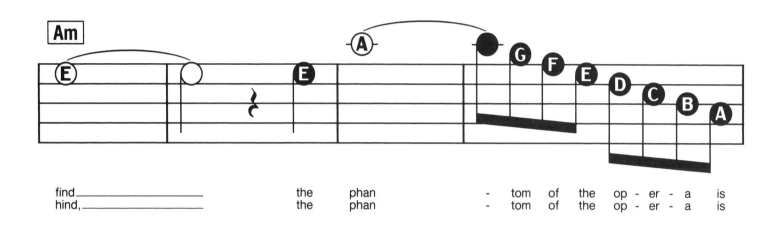

find_____   the   phan   - tom   of   the   op - er - a   is
hind,_____   the   phan   - tom   of   the   op - er - a   is

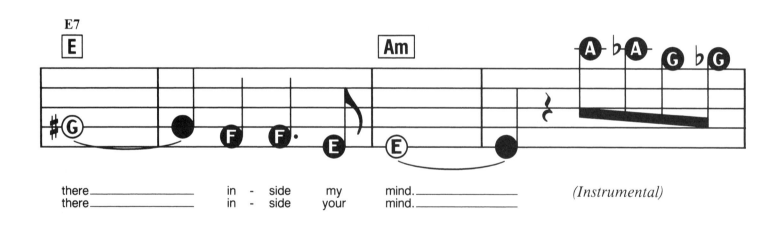

there_____   in - side   my   mind._____   *(Instrumental)*
there_____   in - side   your   mind._____

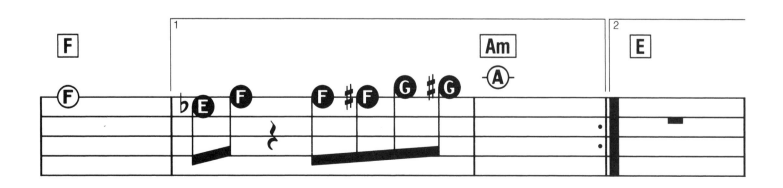

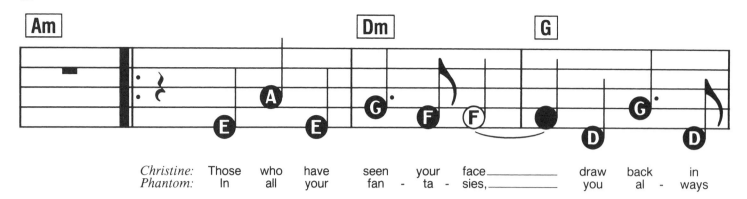

Christine: Those who have seen your face_____ draw back in
Phantom: In all your fan - ta - sies,_____ you al - ways

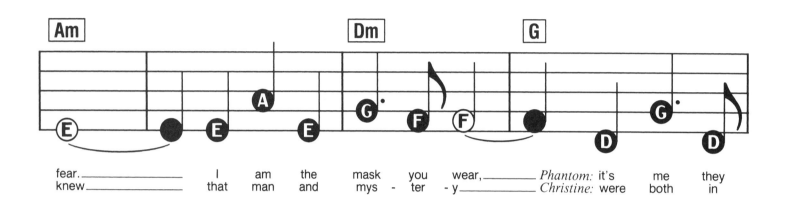

fear._____ I am the mask you wear,_____ Phantom: it's me they
knew_____ that man and mys - ter - y_____ Christine: were both in

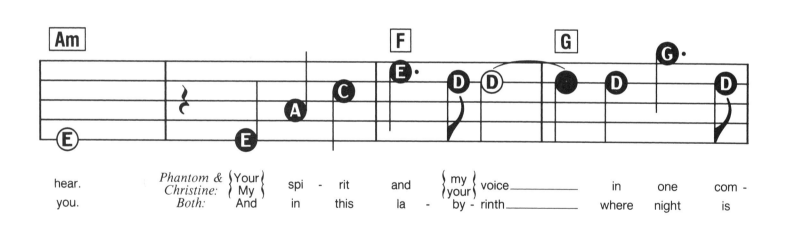

hear. Phantom & {Your} spi - rit and {my} voice_____ in one com -
you. Christine: {My} Both: And in this la - by - rinth_____ where night is

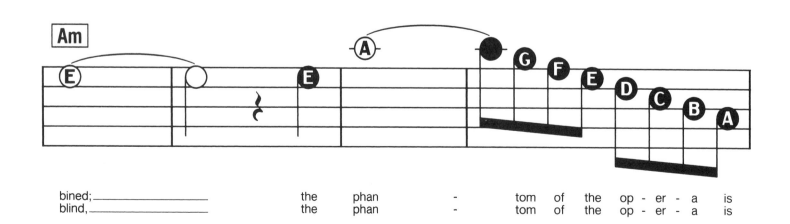

bined;_____ the phan - tom of the op - er - a is
blind,_____ the phan - tom of the op - er - a is

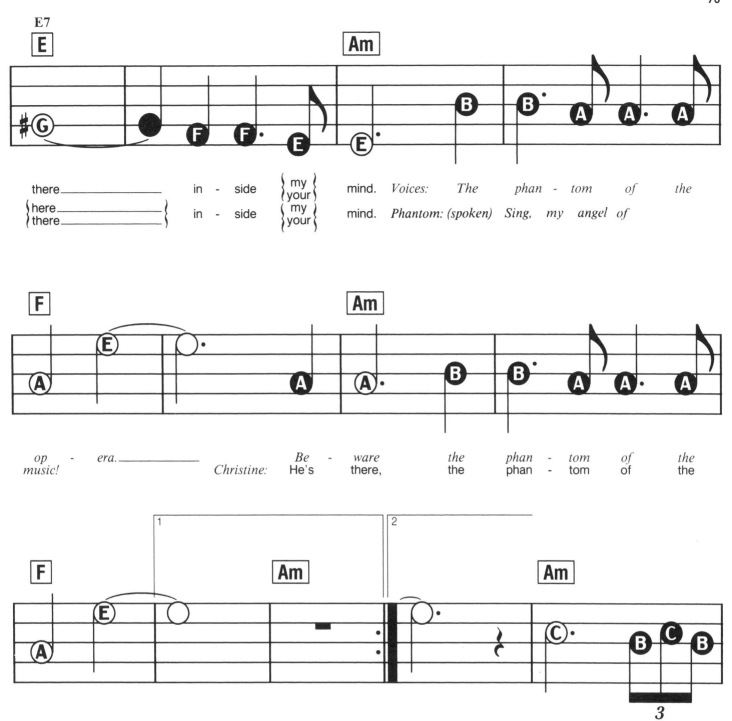

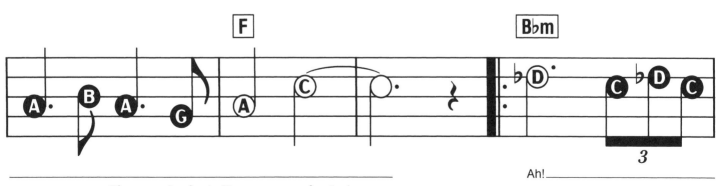

Phantom: (spoken) Sing, my angel, sing!

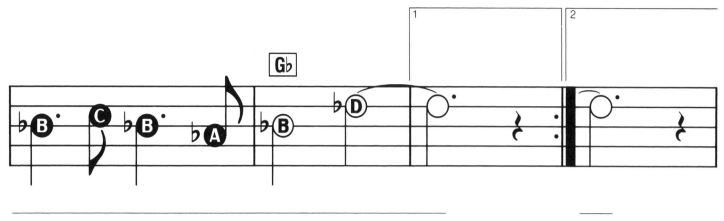

(First time:) Sing for me!

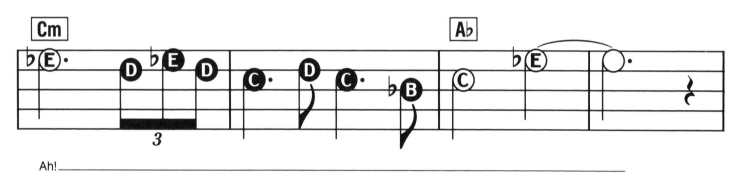

Ah!

Phantom: Sing, my angel of music!

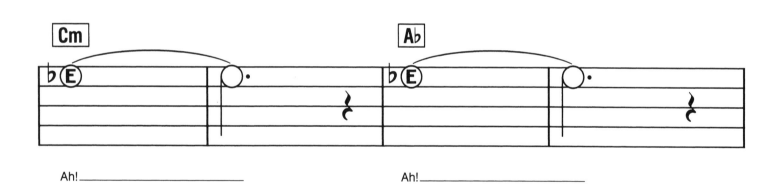

Ah!_____ Ah!_____

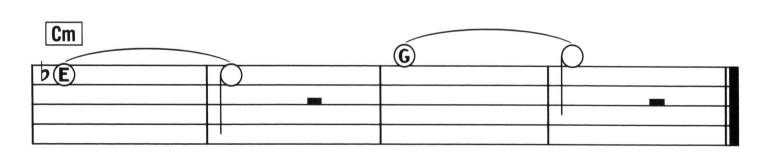

Ah!_____ Ah!_____

Pie Jesu
from REQUIEM

Registration 3
Rhythm: No Rhythm

By Andrew Lloyd Webber

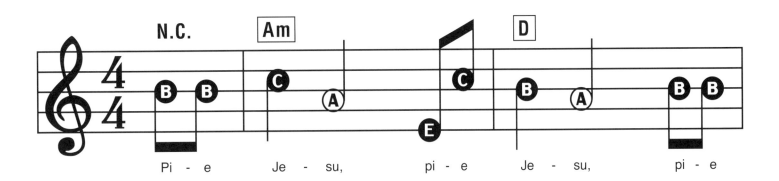

Pi - e   Je - su,   pi - e   Je - su,   pi - e

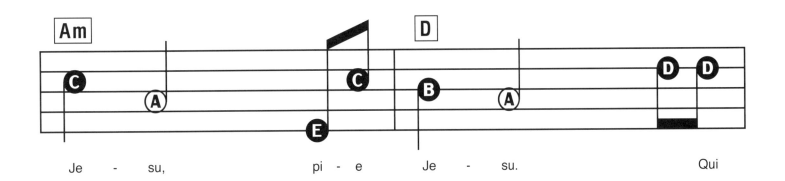

Je - su,   pi - e   Je - su.   Qui

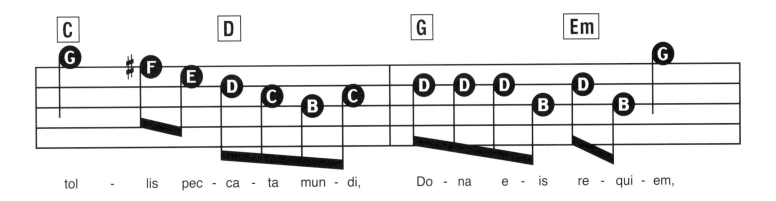

tol - lis pec - ca - ta mun - di,   Do - na e - is re - qui - em,

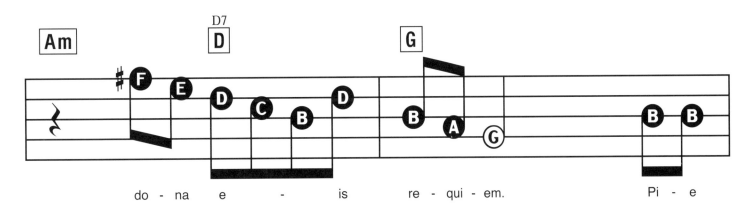

do - na e - is re - qui - em.   Pi - e

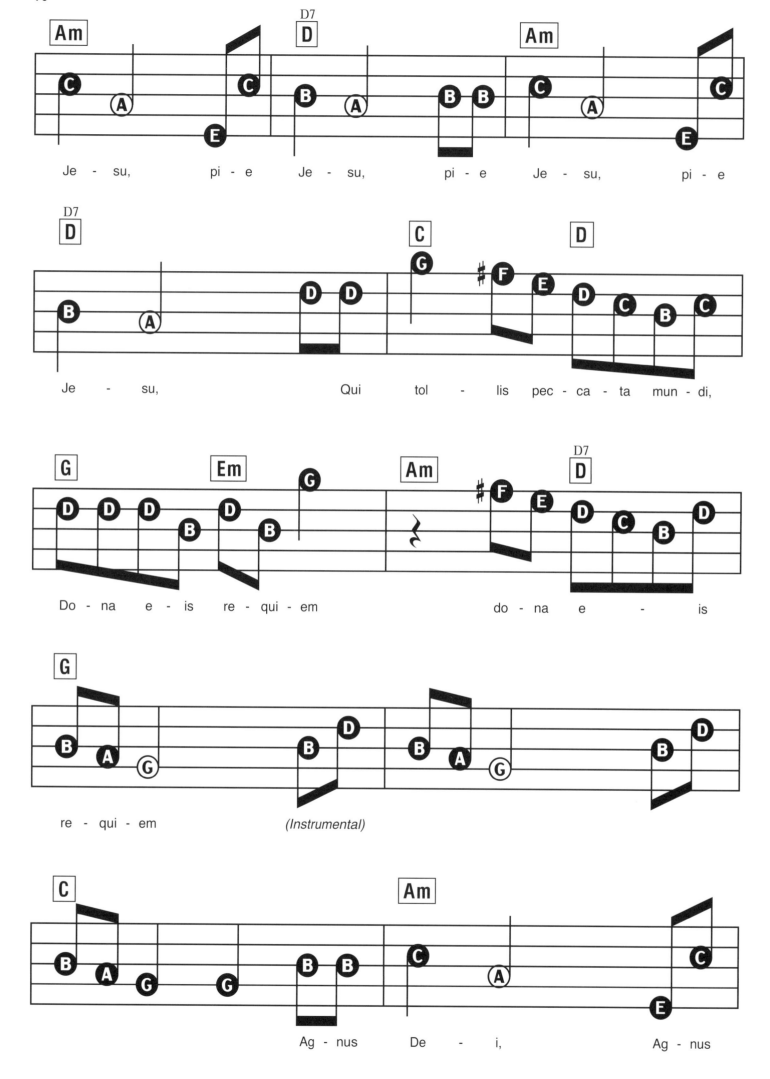

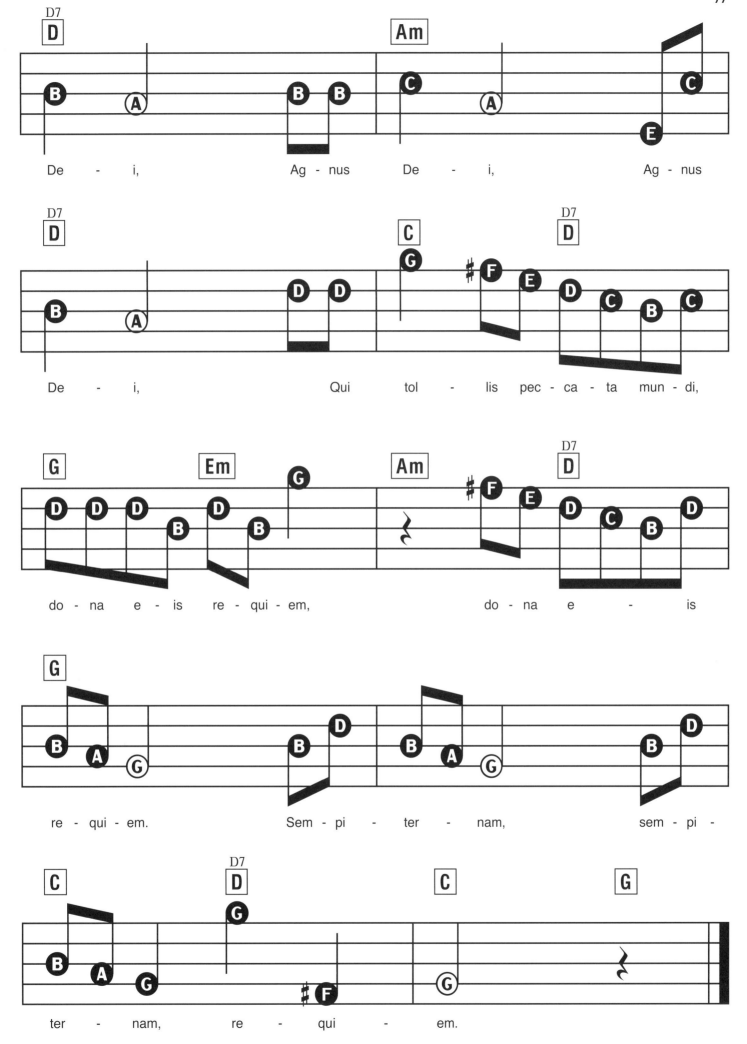

Stick It to the Man
from SCHOOL OF ROCK

Registration 4
Rhythm: Slow Rock or Blues

Music by Andrew Lloyd Webber
Lyrics by Glenn Slater

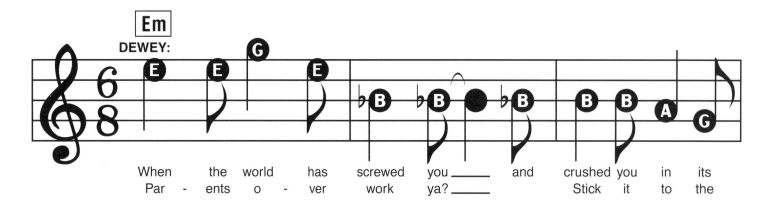

When the world has screwed you _____ and crushed you in its
Par - ents o - ver work ya? _____ Stick it to the

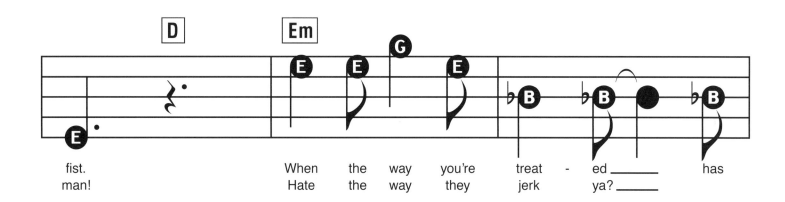

fist. When the way you're treat - ed _____ has
man! Hate the way they jerk ya? _____

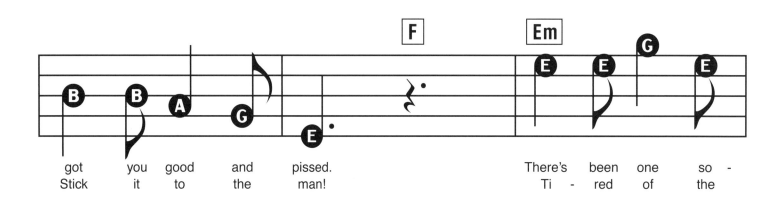

got you good and pissed. There's been one so -
Stick it to the man! Ti - red of the

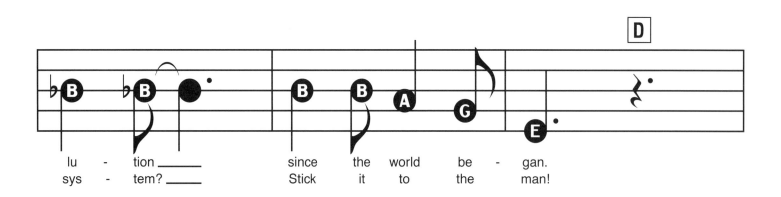

lu - tion _____ since the world be - gan.
sys - tem? _____ Stick it to the man!

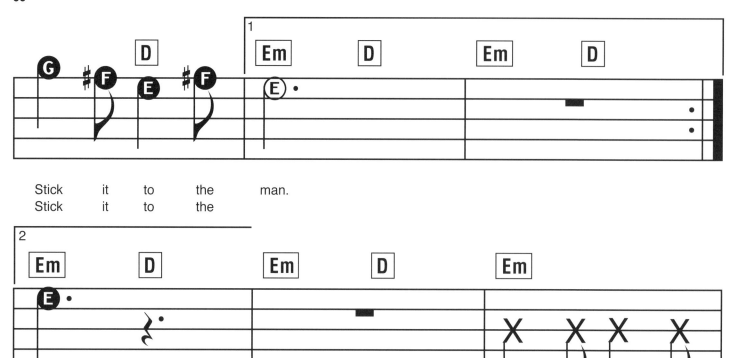

Stick it to the man.
Stick it to the

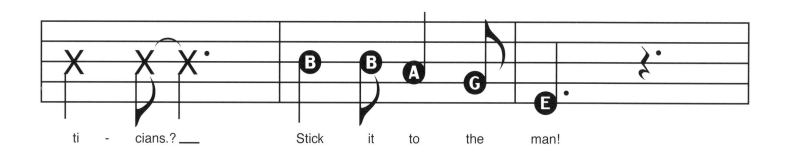

man.   Pissed   at   pol   -   i -

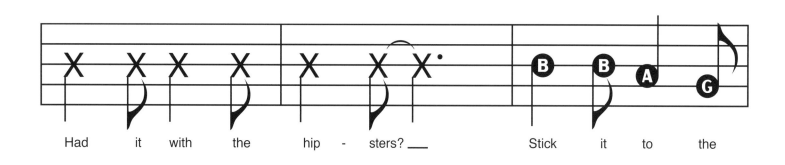

ti   -   cians.? ___   Stick   it   to   the   man!

Had   it   with   the   hip - sters? ___   Stick   it   to   the

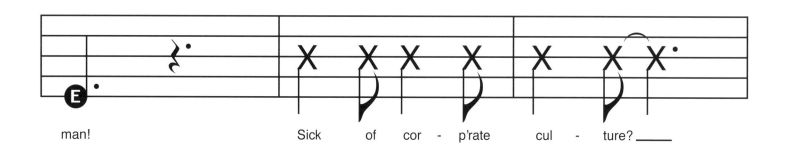

man!   Sick   of   cor - p'rate   cul   -   ture? _____

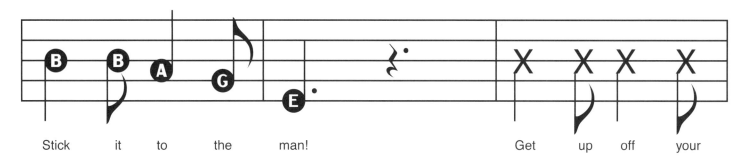

Stick it to the man! Get up off your

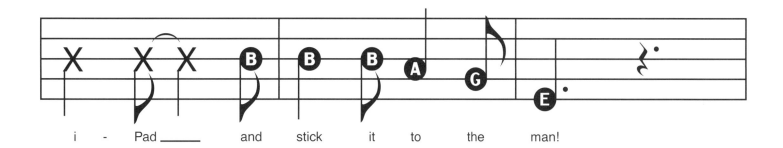

i - Pad _____ and stick it to the man!

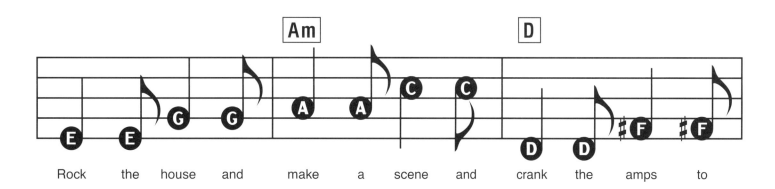

Rock the house and make a scene and crank the amps to

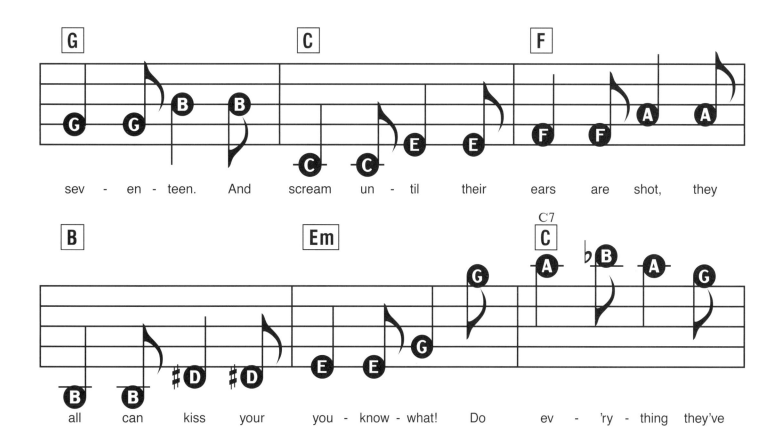

sev - en - teen. And scream un - til their ears are shot, they

all can kiss your you - know - what! Do ev - 'ry - thing they've

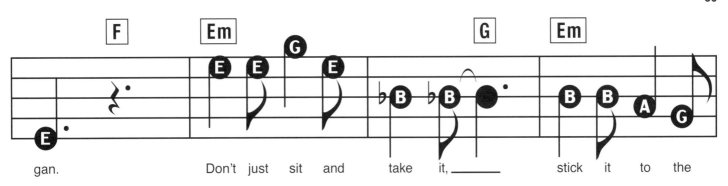

gan.   Don't just sit and take it, _____ stick it to the

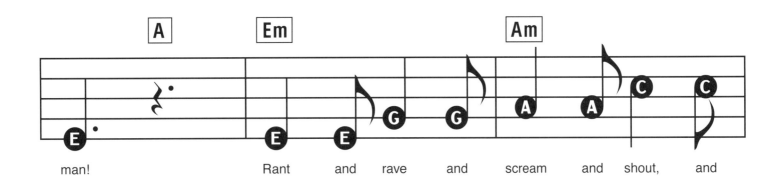

man!   Rant and rave and scream and shout, and

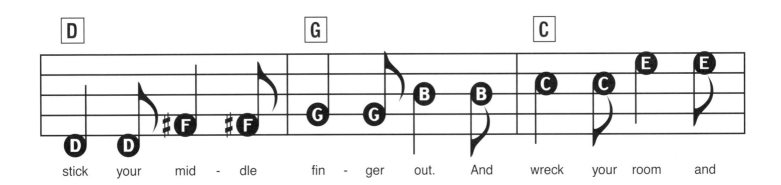

stick your mid - dle fin - ger out.   And wreck your room and

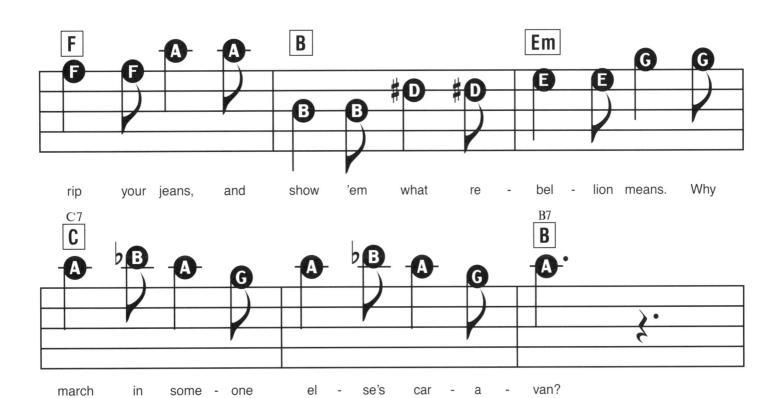

rip your jeans, and show 'em what re - bel - lion means. Why

march in some - one el - se's car - a - van?

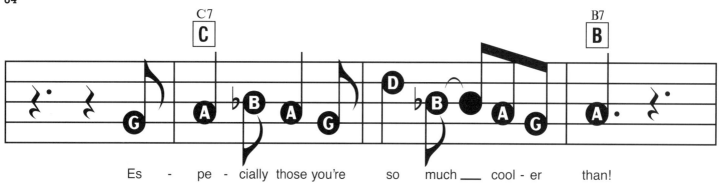

Es - pe - cially those you're so much __ cool - er than!

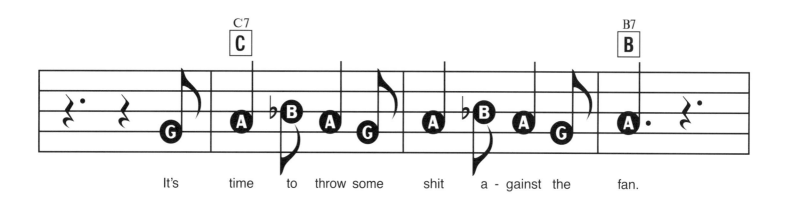

It's time to throw some shit a - gainst the fan.

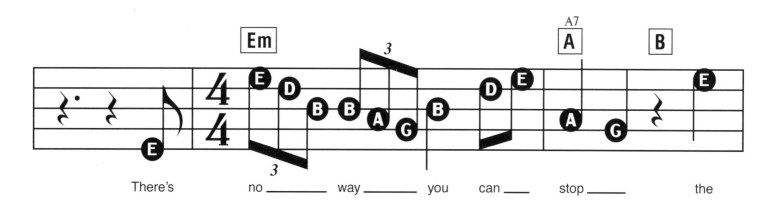

There's no _____ way _____ you can __ stop _____ the

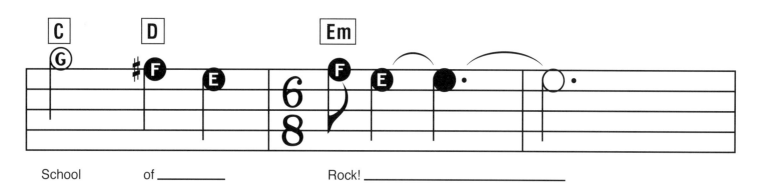

School of _____ Rock! _____

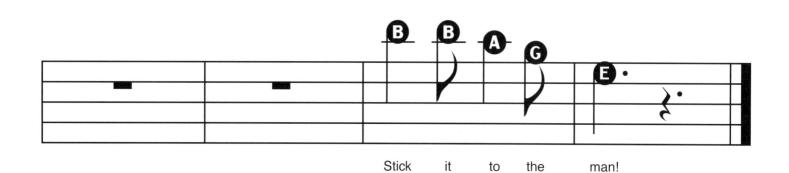

Stick it to the man!

Superstar
from JESUS CHRIST SUPERSTAR

Registration 9
Rhythm: Rock or Jazz Rock

Words by Tim Rice
Music by Andrew Lloyd Webber

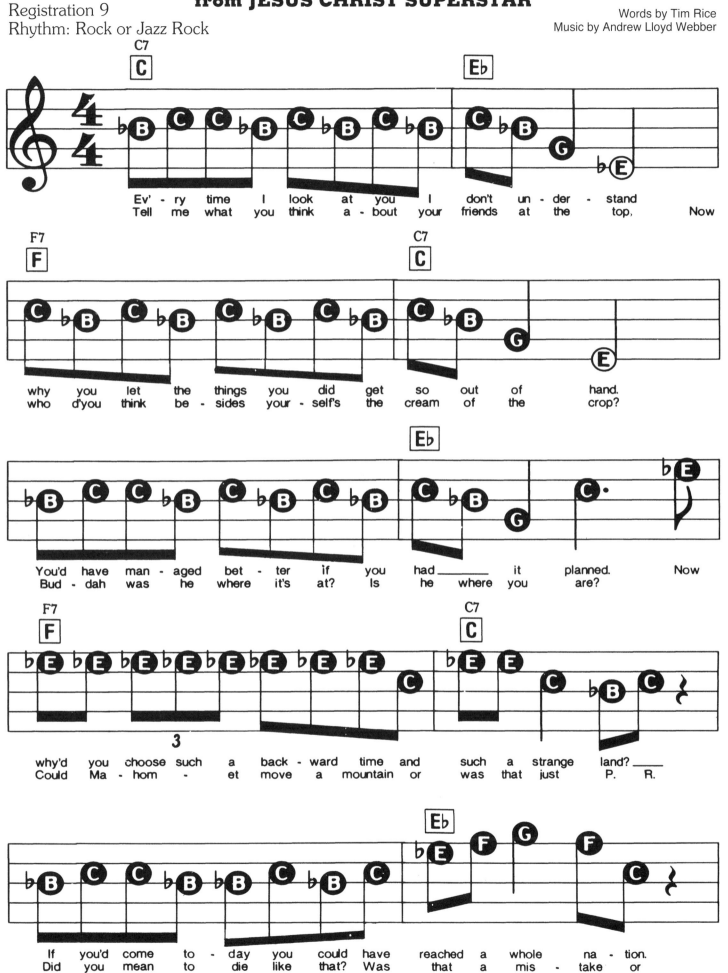

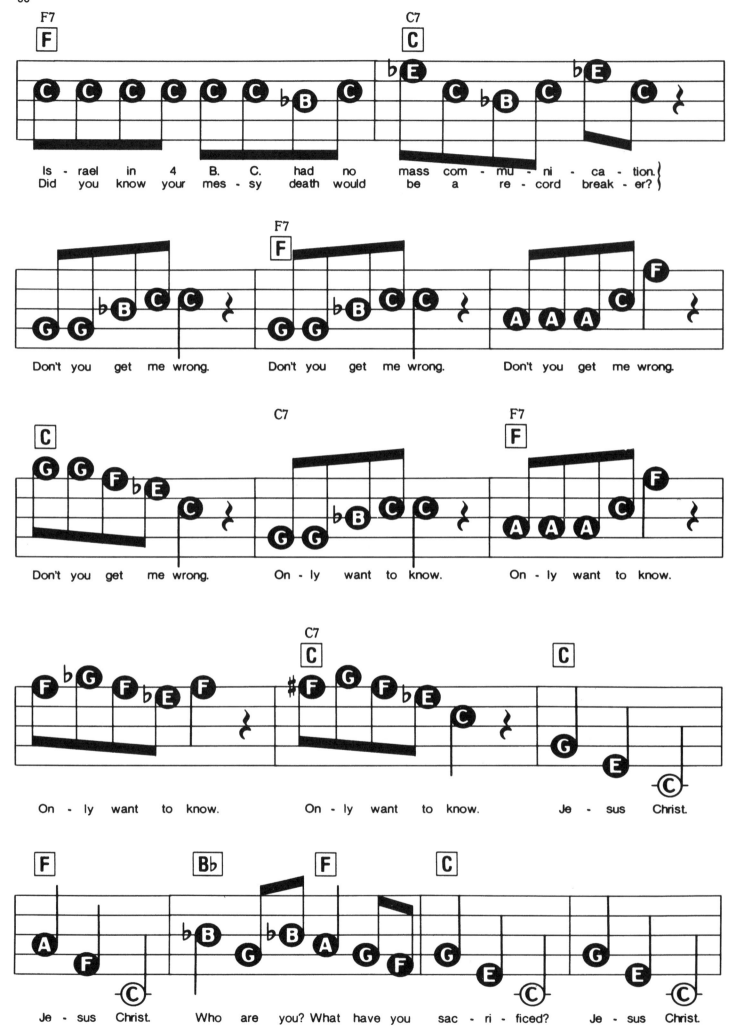

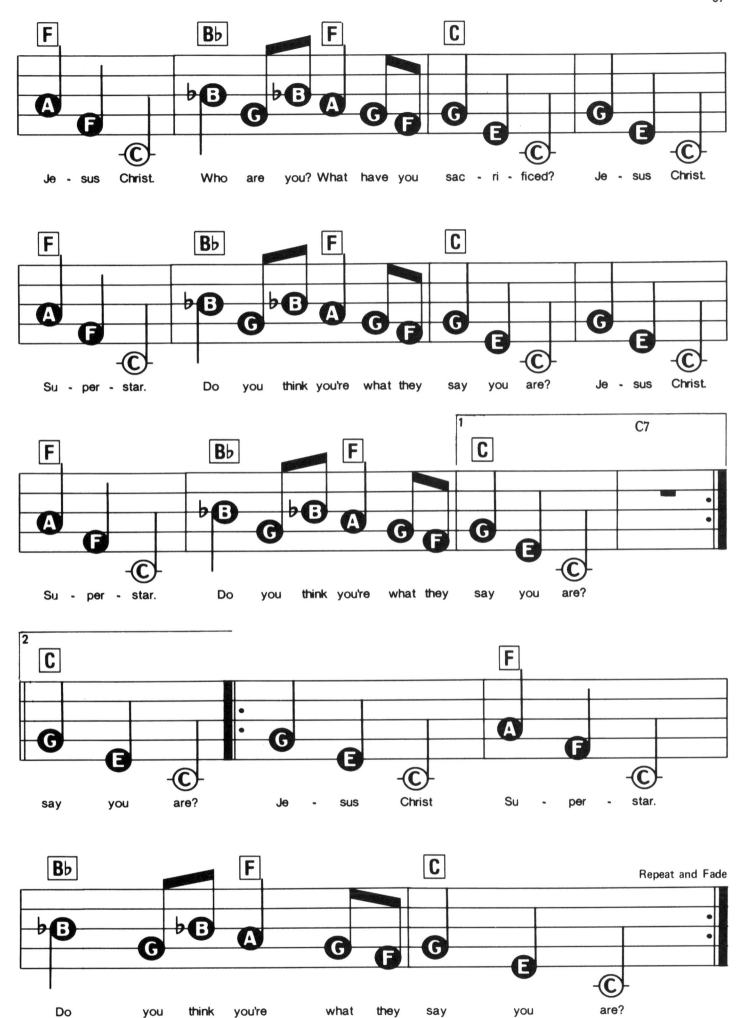

Tell Me on a Sunday
from SONG & DANCE

Registration 9
Rhythm: Pops or 8-Beat

Music by Andrew Lloyd Webber
Lyrics by Don Black

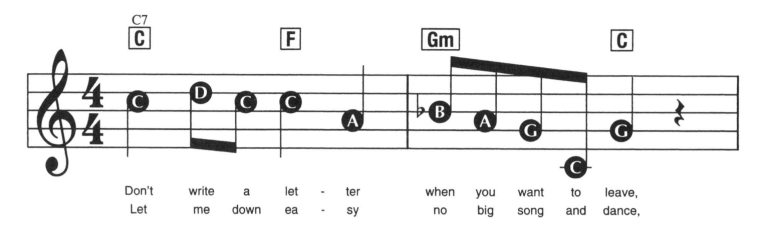

Don't write a let - ter when you want to leave,
Let me down ea - sy no big song and dance,

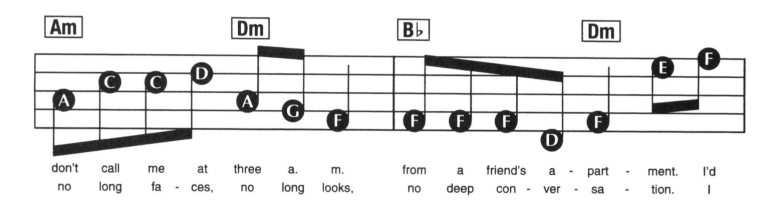

don't call me at three a. m. from a friend's a - part - ment. I'd
no long fa - ces, no long looks, no deep con - ver - sa - tion. I

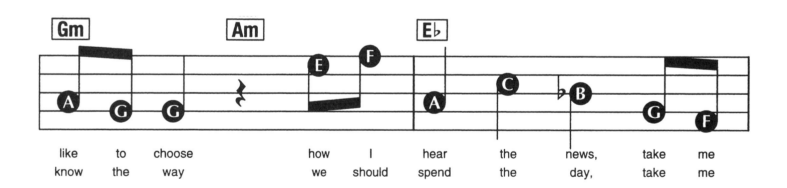

like to choose how I hear the news, take me
know the way we should spend the day, take me

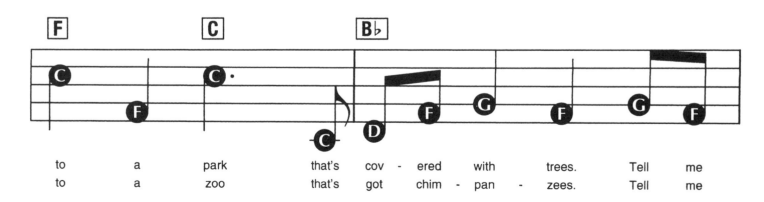

to a park that's cov - ered with trees. Tell me
to a zoo that's got chim - pan - zees. Tell me

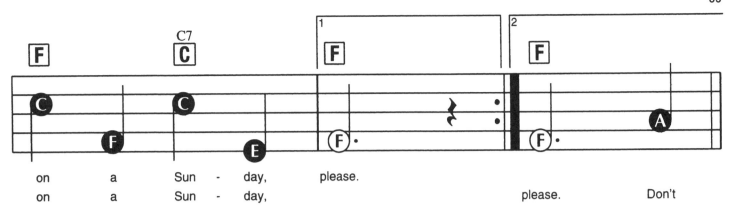

on a Sun - day, please.
on a Sun - day, please. Don't

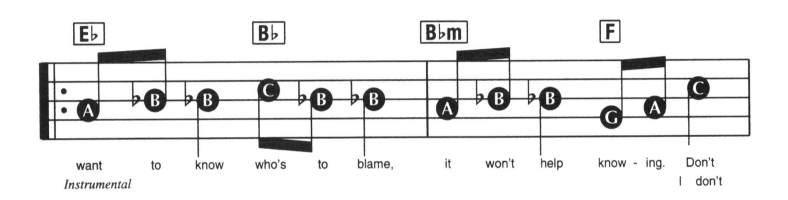

want to know who's to blame, it won't help know - ing. Don't
Instrumental   I don't

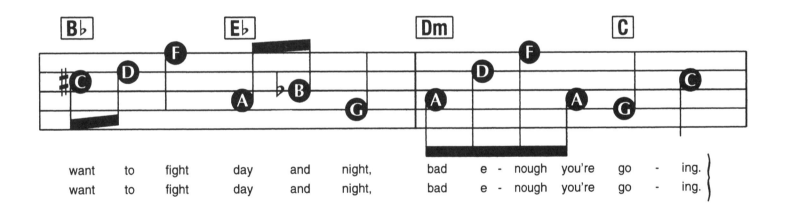

want to fight day and night, bad e - nough you're go - ing.
want to fight day and night, bad e - nough you're go - ing.

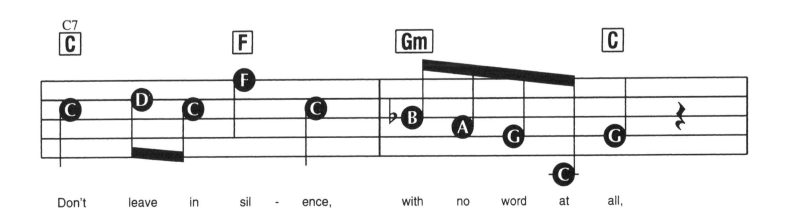

Don't leave in sil - ence, with no word at all,

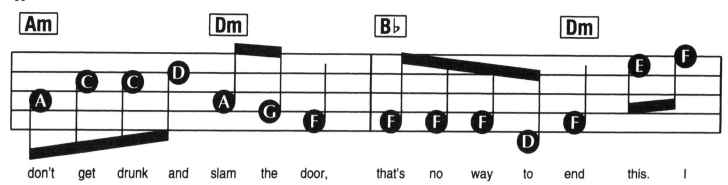

don't get drunk and slam the door, that's no way to end this. I

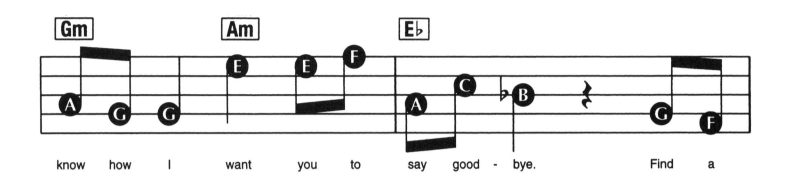

know how I want you to say good - bye. Find a

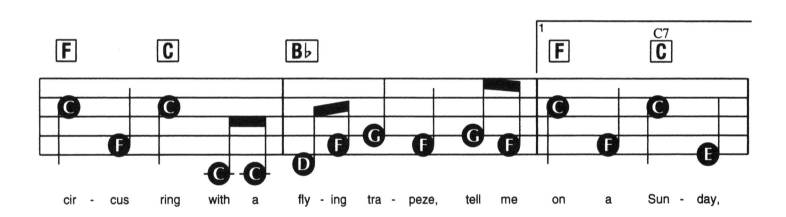

cir - cus ring with a fly - ing tra - peze, tell me on a Sun - day,

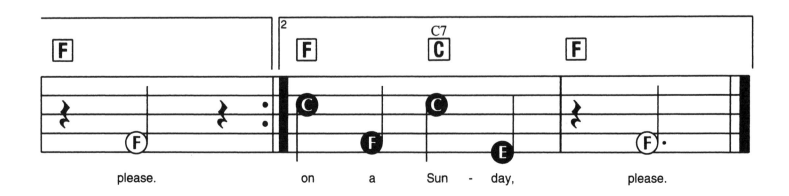

please. on a Sun - day, please.

You Must Love Me

from the Cinergi Motion Picture EVITA

Registration 1
Rhythm: Pops

Words by Tim Rice
Music by Andrew Lloyd Webber

C **G** **C**

E E E G G· B C

Where do we go from here?
(Instrumental)

C7
C **F**

E E E G ♭B ♭B ♭B A ♭B A

This is - n't where we in - tend - ed to be.

Dm

F E F A F E E D E F C C

We had it all, you be - lieved ___ in me, I be -

G **C** **G**

C D C D E E E G B

lieved ___ in you.   Cer - tain - ties   dis - ap -
End instrumental   *Sung:* Why are you   at my

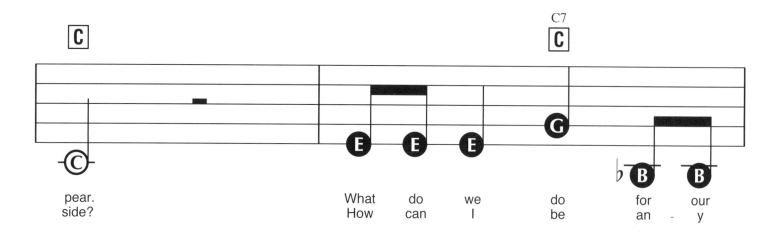

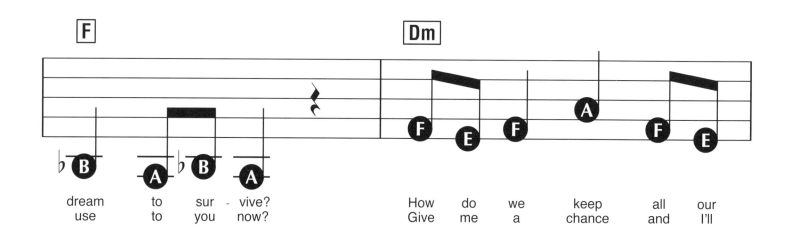

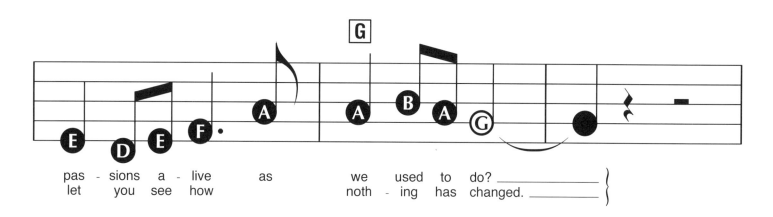

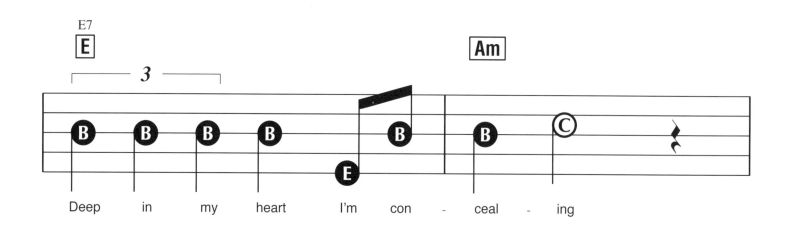

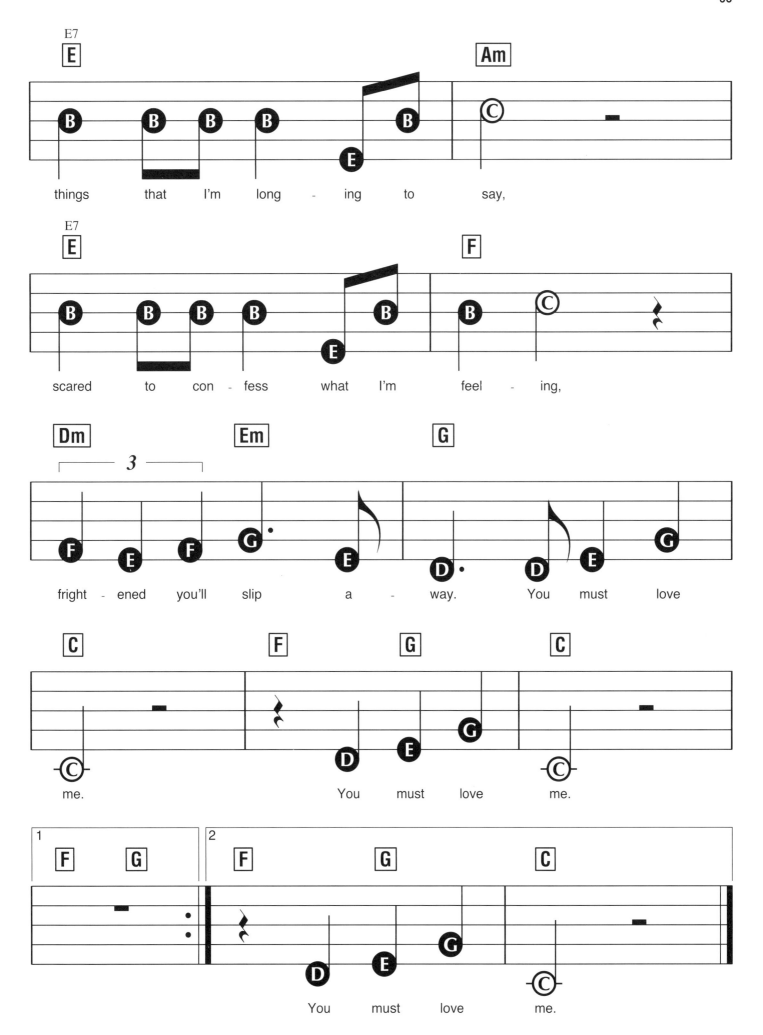

Whistle Down the Wind
from WHISTLE DOWN THE WIND

Registration 1
Rhythm: Fox Trot

Music by Andrew Lloyd Webber
Lyrics by Jim Steinman

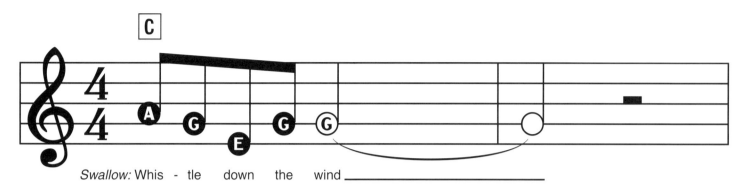

Swallow: Whis - tle down the wind _____

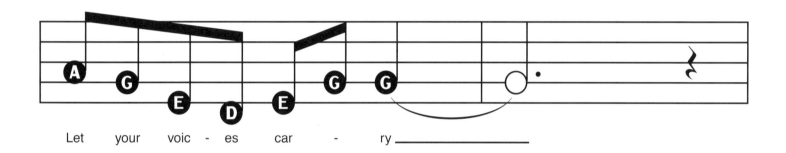

Let your voic - es car - ry _____

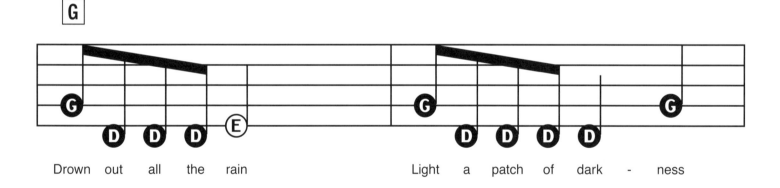

Drown out all the rain   Light a patch of dark - ness

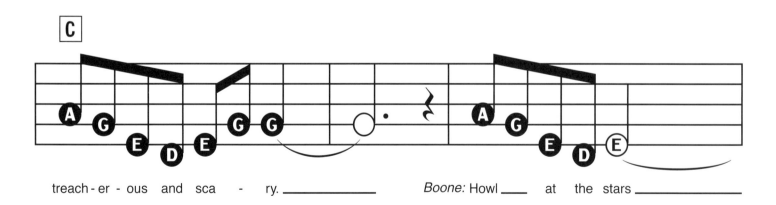

treach - er - ous and sca - ry. _____   Boone: Howl ____ at the stars _____

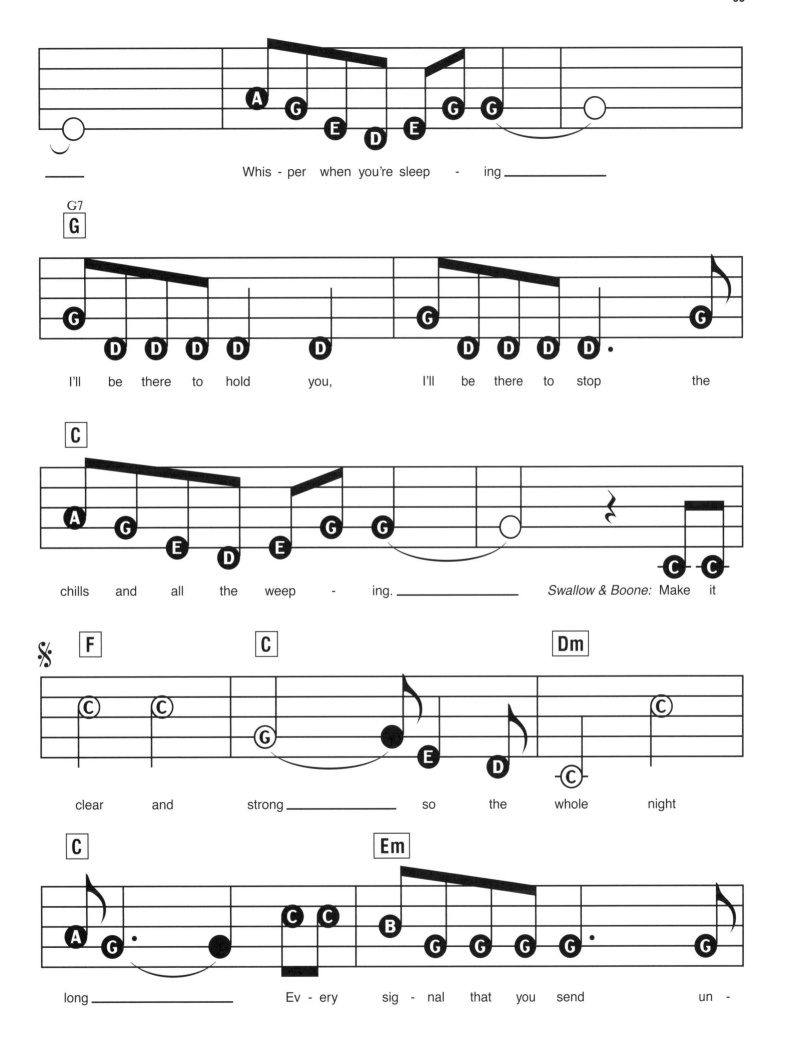

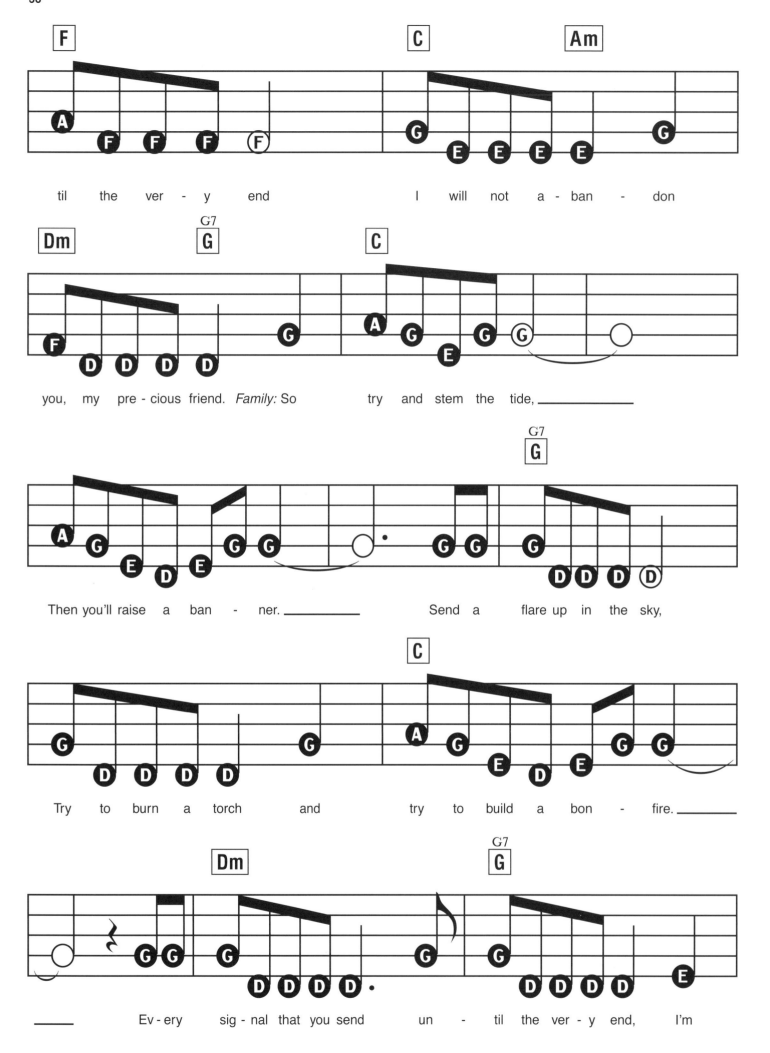

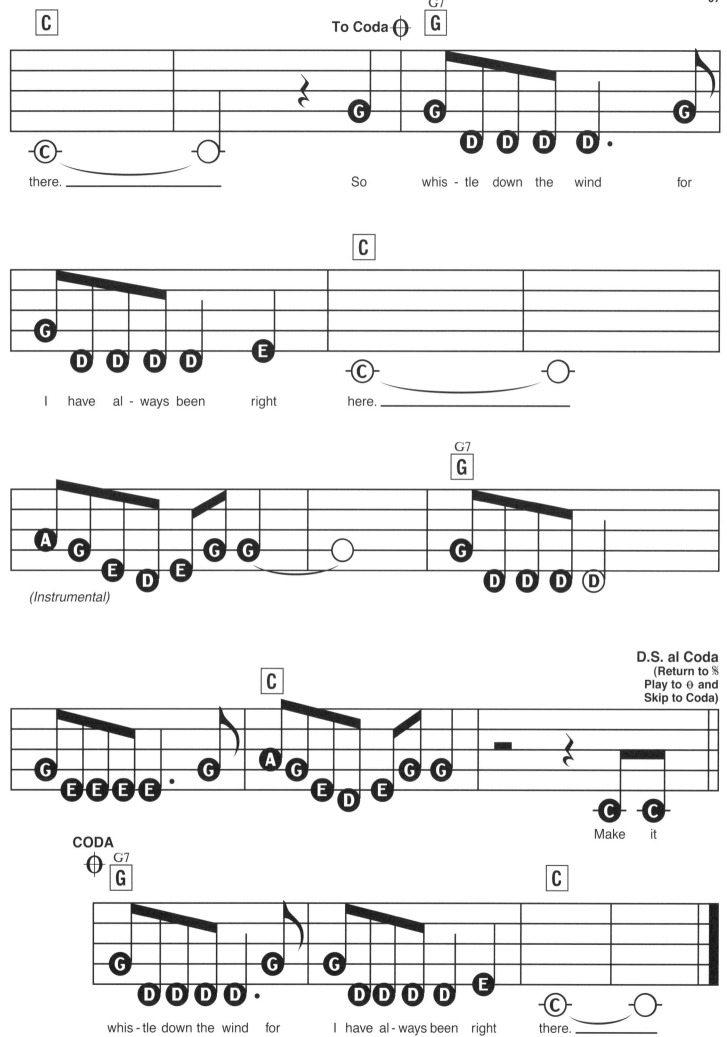

You're in the Band
from SCHOOL OF ROCK

Registration 4
Rhythm: Rock or Pop

Music by Andrew Lloyd Webber
Lyrics by Glenn Slater

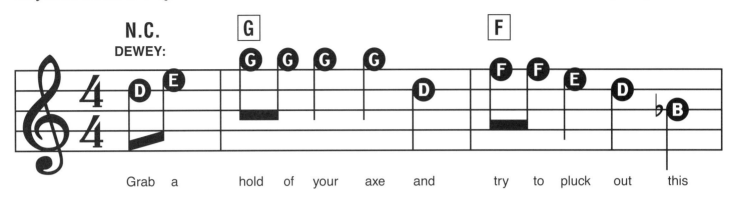

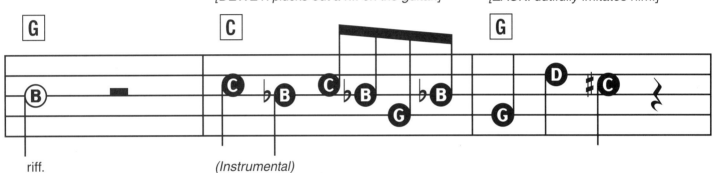

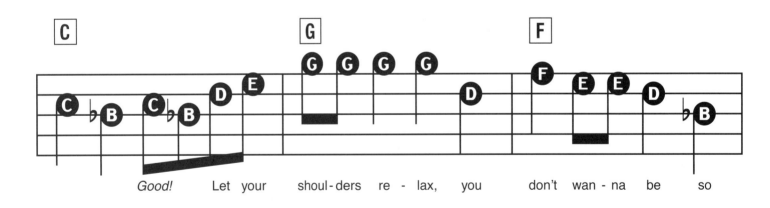

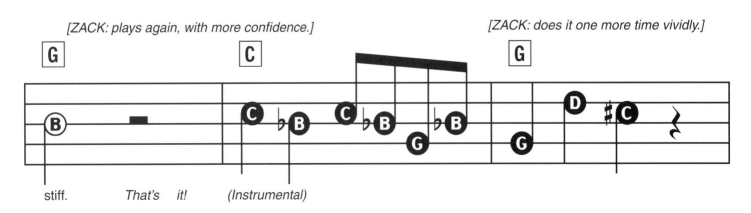

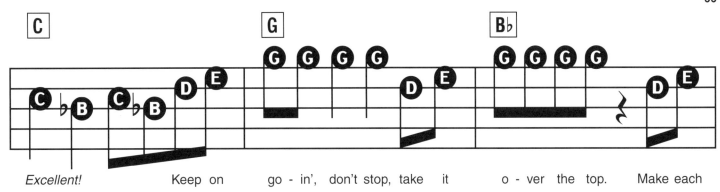

Excellent! Keep on go - in', don't stop, take it o - ver the top. Make each

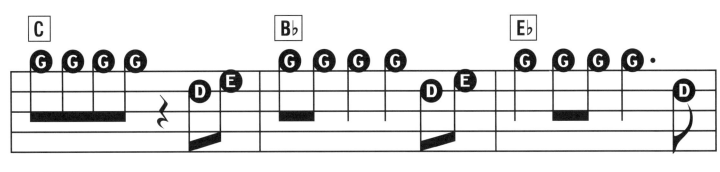

note real - ly pop, squeeze out ev - 'ry last drop. Give it one fi - nal whop! And

yes! You're in the band. _____

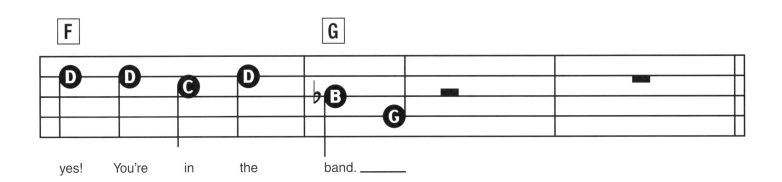

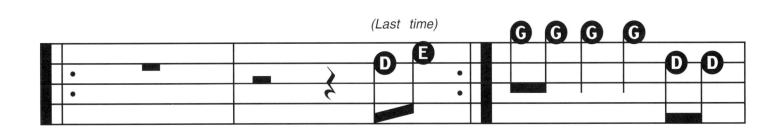

(Last time)

Turn a cel - lo this way, and it's

[DEWEY: points to KATIE.]

DEWEY: You! What's your name?
KATIE: Kate.
DEWEY: And what is that big, lumpy thing
      you were playing?
KATIE: The cello?
DEWEY: The cheel- lo. Right. Come here.

[He picks up a bass guitar by the neck,
then tilts it onto its side.]

100

[He plays the riff of "Smoke on the Water." Then he passes it to KATIE.]

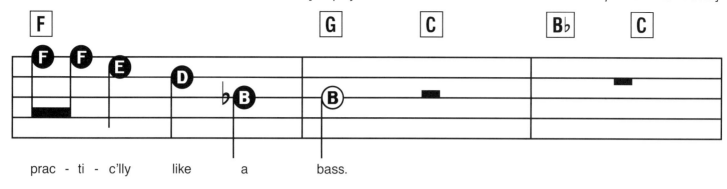

prac - ti - c'lly   like   a   bass.

Pop   the   strings when   you   play   and

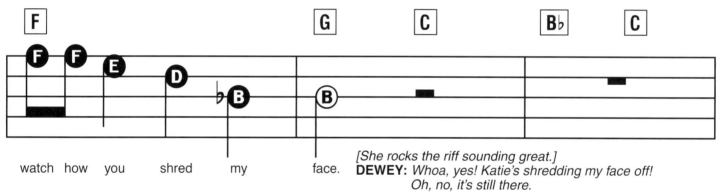

watch   how   you   shred   my   face.

[She rocks the riff sounding great.]
DEWEY: *Whoa, yes! Katie's shredding my face off!*
Oh, no, it's still there.
[KATIE: now plays along to the music.]

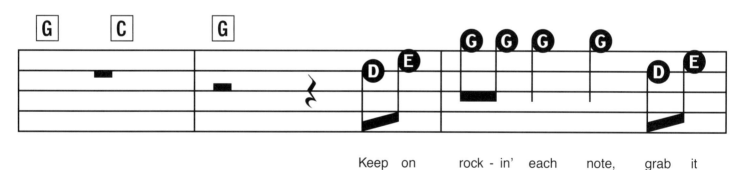

Keep   on   rock - in' each   note,   grab   it

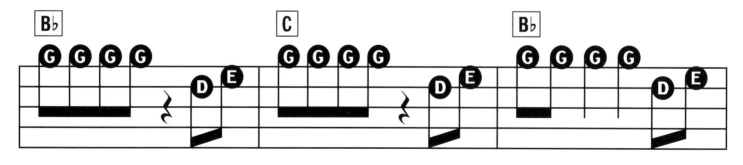

right   by   the throat.   Keep the   rhy - thm a - float,   don't for - get   to   e - mote! And that's

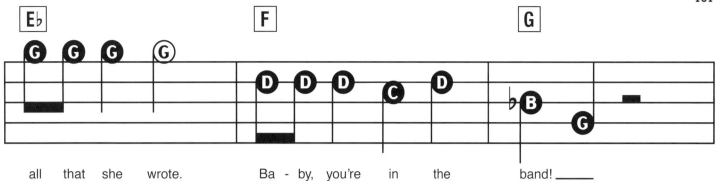

all that she wrote. Ba - by, you're in the band! _____

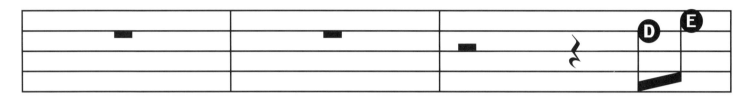

[Next he turns to LAWRENCE.]
DEWEY: *Piano man!*
LAWRENCE: *Lawrence.*
DEWEY: *Whatever, dude, come here!*

If you

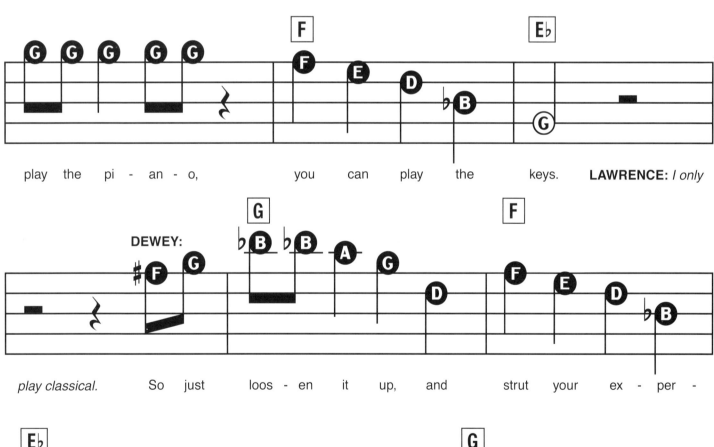

play the pi - an - o, you can play the keys. **LAWRENCE:** *I only*

play classical. So just loos - en it up, and strut your ex - per -

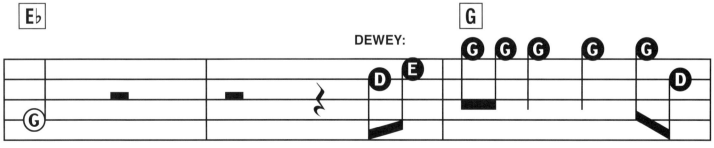

tise. **LAWRENCE:** *I don't think I can.* Take a look at this mu - sic and

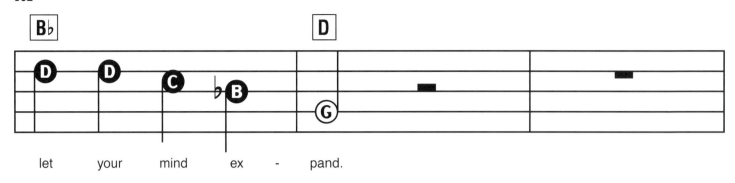

let   your   mind   ex -   pand.

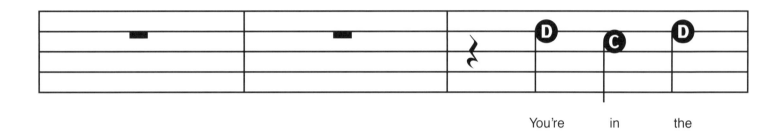

You're   in   the

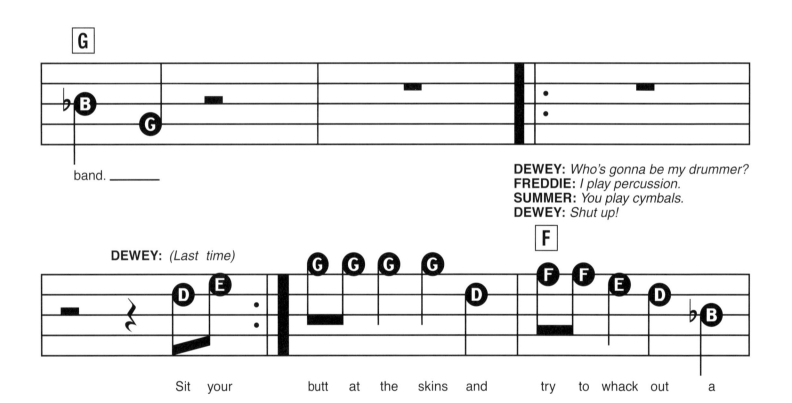

band. _____

DEWEY: *Who's gonna be my drummer?*
FREDDIE: *I play percussion.*
SUMMER: *You play cymbals.*
DEWEY: *Shut up!*

DEWEY: *(Last time)*

Sit   your   butt   at   the   skins and   try to whack out   a

[FREDDIE: sits at the drum kit, finds a simple rhythm.]

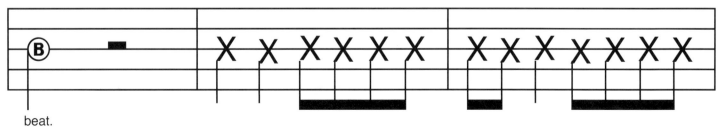

beat.

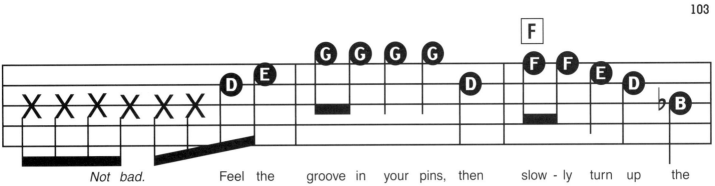

Not bad. Feel the groove in your pins, then slow - ly turn up the

G *[FREDDIE: getting the hang of it, starts getting fancy.]*

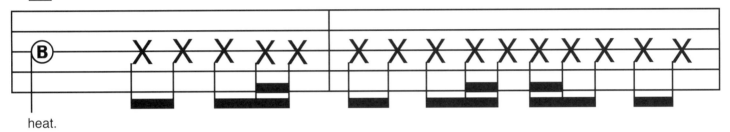

heat.

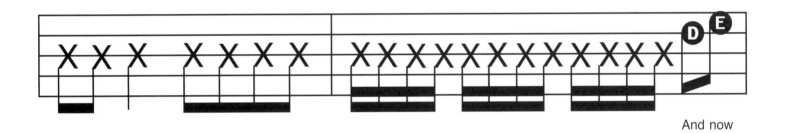

And now

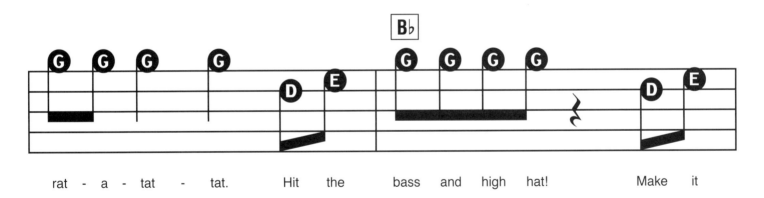

rat - a - tat - tat. Hit the bass and high hat! Make it

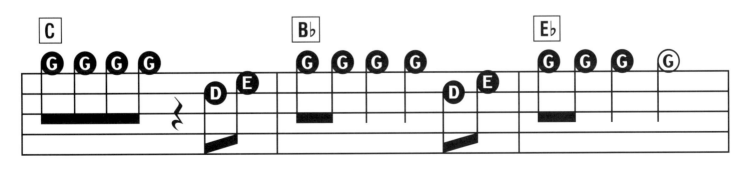

juic - y and fat! Yeah, ex - act - ly like that! And now shut it down flat...

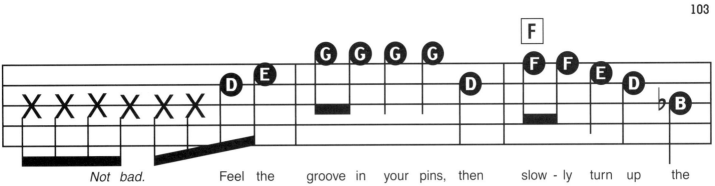

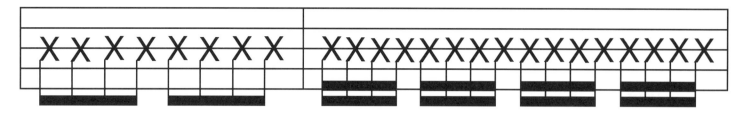

F *[FREDDIE: plays a monster drum fill…]*

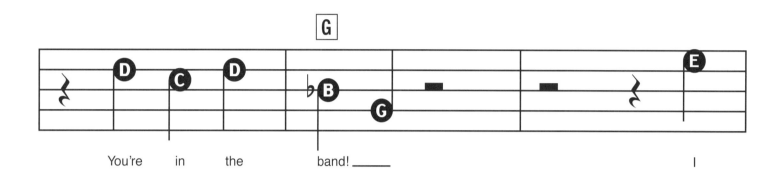

G

You're in the band! _____ I

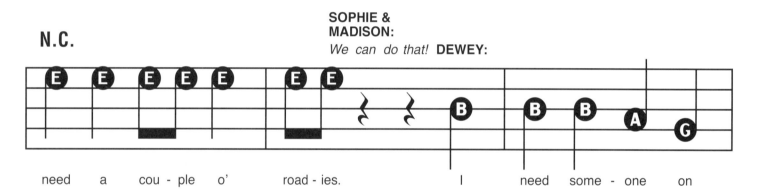

N.C.

SOPHIE & MADISON: *We can do that!* **DEWEY:**

need a cou - ple o' road - ies. I need some - one on

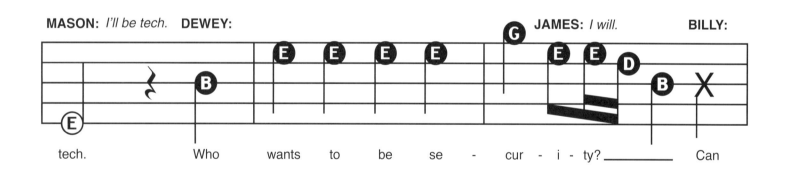

MASON: *I'll be tech.* **DEWEY:** **JAMES:** *I will.* **BILLY:**

tech. Who wants to be se - cur - i - ty? _____ Can

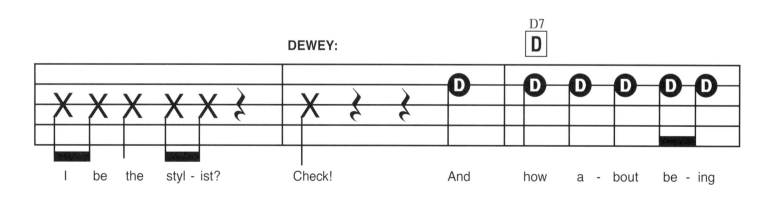

DEWEY:

D7 **D**

I be the styl - ist? Check! And how a - bout be - ing

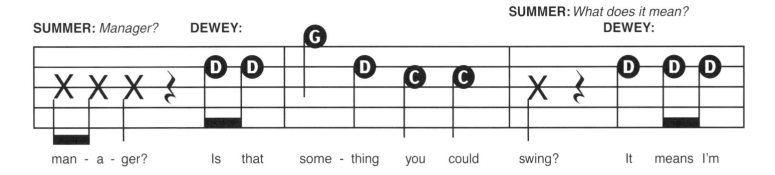

SUMMER: *Manager?*   DEWEY: SUMMER: *What does it mean?*   DEWEY:

man - a - ger?   Is   that   some - thing   you   could   swing?   It   means I'm

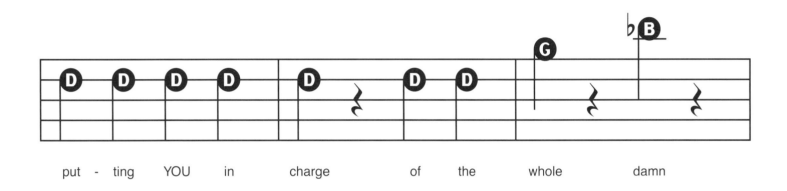

put - ting   YOU   in   charge   of   the   whole   damn

[All instruments drop out except the drums, played by FREDDIE.]

N.C.

SUMMER: *[Pumping fist]*   DEWEY:

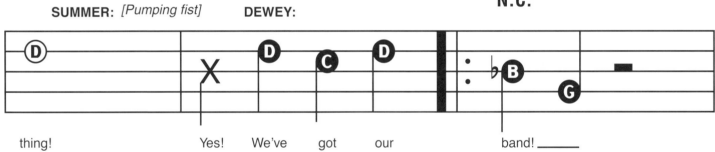

thing!   Yes!   We've   got   our   band! _____

G

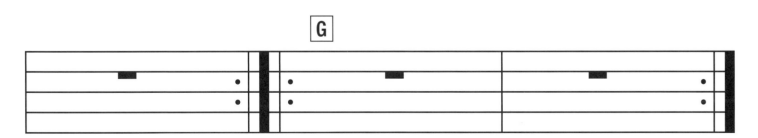

DEWEY *(2nd time): Now, Freddie,*
keep that beat going.
Katie, come in on G…

DEWEY *(2nd time): Awesome!*
Lawrence, take me to the moon!

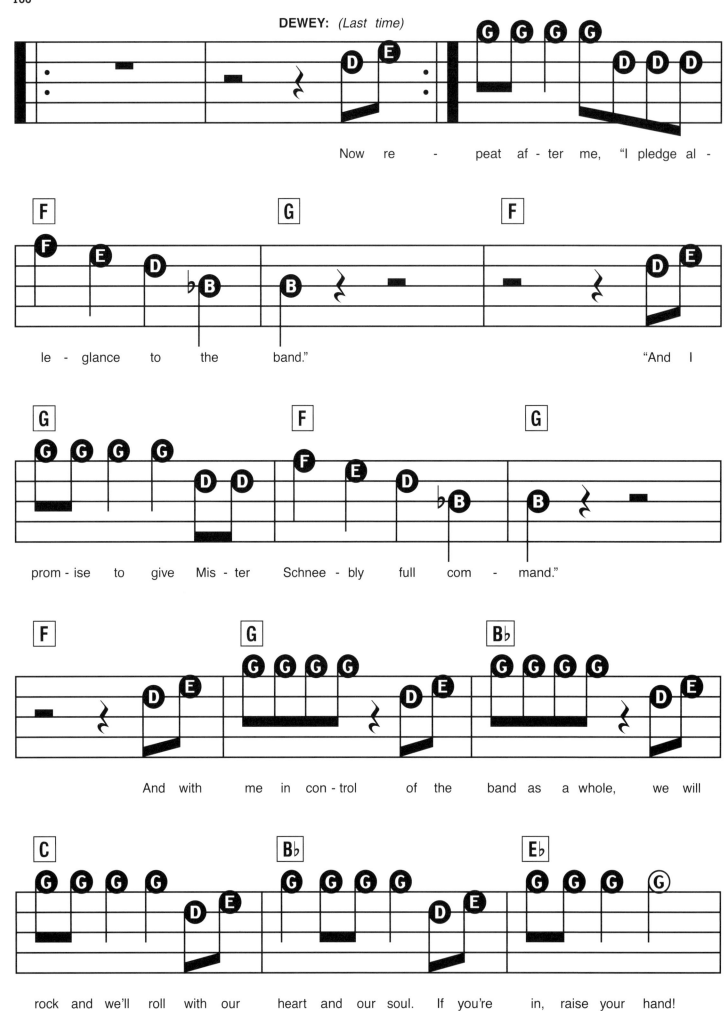

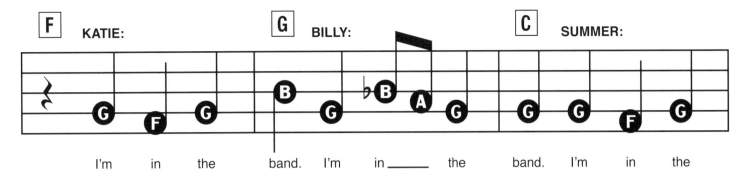

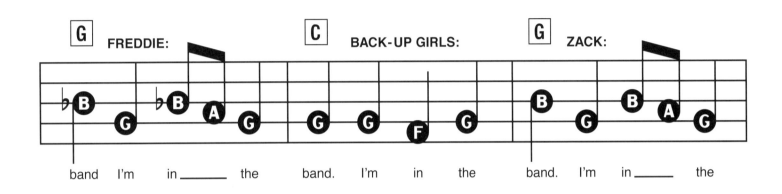

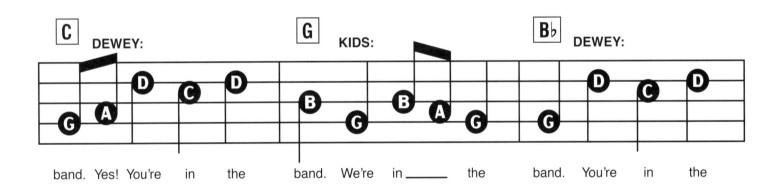

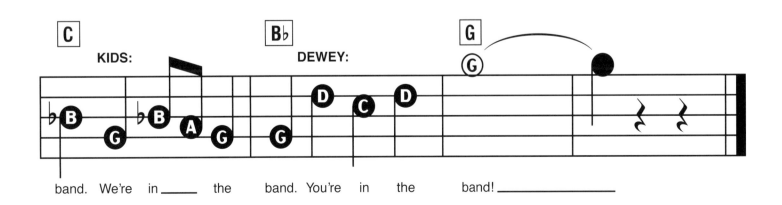

'Til I Hear You Sing
from LOVE NEVER DIES

Registration 2
Rhythm: None

Music by Andrew Lloyd Webber
Lyrics by Glenn Slater

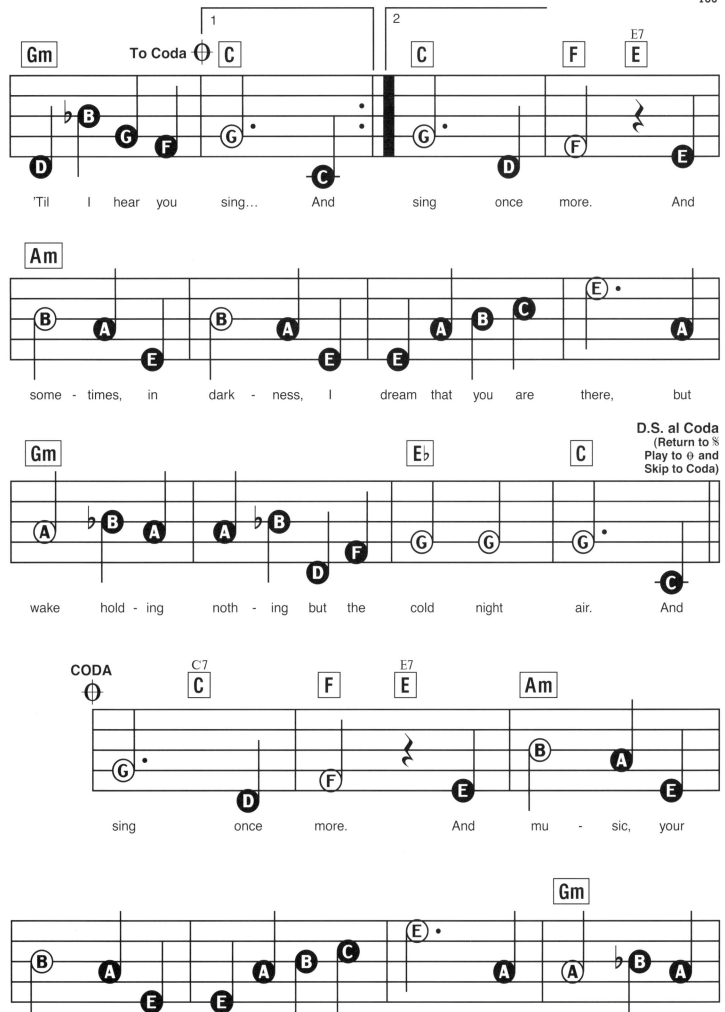

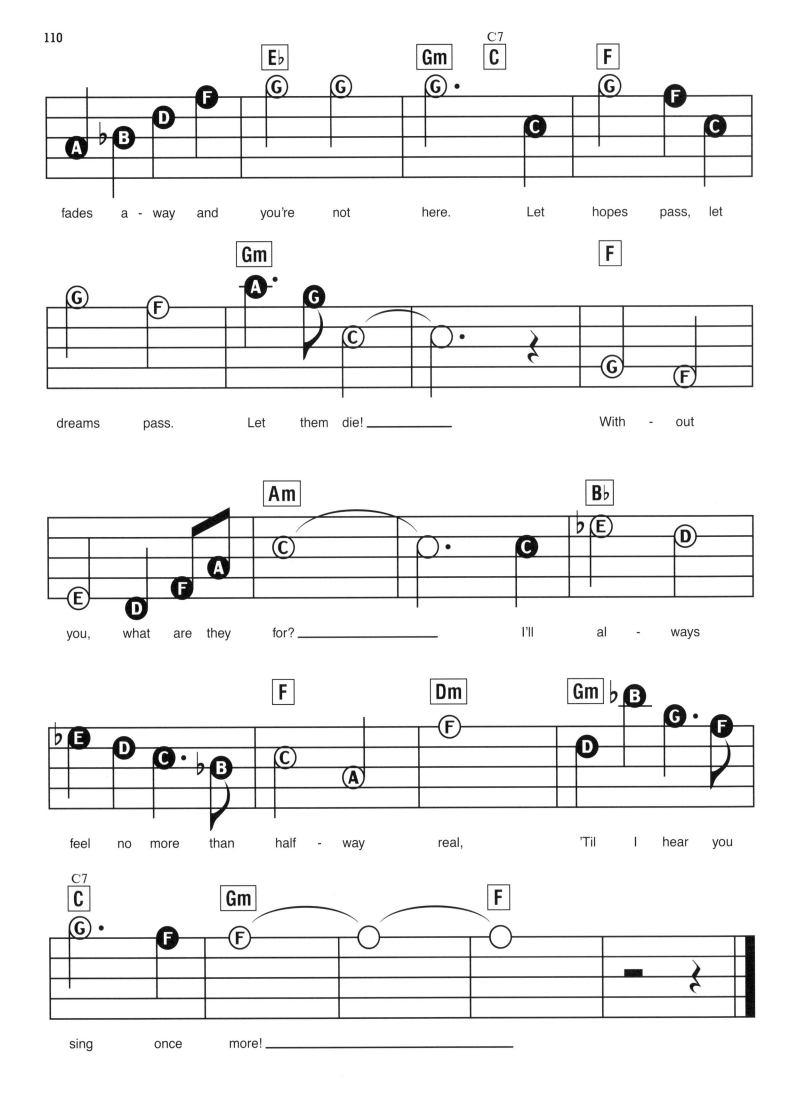

 # Registration Guide

- Match the Registration number on the song to the corresponding numbered category below. Select and activate an instrumental sound available on your instrument.

- Choose an automatic rhythm appropriate to the mood and style of the song. (Consult your Owner's Guide for proper operation of automatic rhythm features.)

- Adjust the tempo and volume controls to comfortable settings.

Registration

1	Mellow	Flutes, Clarinet, Oboe, Flugel Horn, Trombone, French Horn, Organ Flutes
2	Ensemble	Brass Section, Sax Section, Wind Ensemble, Full Organ, Theater Organ
3	Strings	Violin, Viola, Cello, Fiddle, String Ensemble, Pizzicato, Organ Strings
4	Guitars	Acoustic/Electric Guitars, Banjo, Mandolin, Dulcimer, Ukulele, Hawaiian Guitar
5	Mallets	Vibraphone, Marimba, Xylophone, Steel Drums, Bells, Celesta, Chimes
6	Liturgical	Pipe Organ, Hand Bells, Vocal Ensemble, Choir, Organ Flutes
7	Bright	Saxophones, Trumpet, Mute Trumpet, Synth Leads, Jazz/Gospel Organs
8	Piano	Piano, Electric Piano, Honky Tonk Piano, Harpsichord, Clavi
9	Novelty	Melodic Percussion, Wah Trumpet, Synth, Whistle, Kazoo, Perc. Organ
10	Bellows	Accordion, French Accordion, Mussette, Harmonica, Pump Organ, Bagpipes

FOR ORGANS, PIANOS & ELECTRONIC KEYBOARDS

E-Z PLAY® TODAY PUBLICATIONS

The E-Z Play® Today songbook series is the shortest distance between beginning music and playing fun! Check out this list of highlights and visit www.halleonard.com for a complete listing of all volumes and songlists.

HAL•LEONARD

Prices, contents, and availability subject to change without notice